FOUNDATIONS OF CRIMINAL JUSTICE

FOUNDATIONS OF CRIMINAL JUSTICE

ONE MORE CHANCE

BY

LEWIS E. MacBRAYNE

and

JAMES P. RAMSAY

with a new introduction by

H. Bruce Pierce

AMS PRESS INC.

NEW YORK

LONDON   TORONTO

1973

ONE MORE CHANCE

An Experiment in Human Salvage

BY

LEWIS E. MacBRAYNE

AND

JAMES P. RAMSAY

BOSTON
SMALL, MAYNARD & COMPANY
PUBLISHERS

HV 9305
M4 M2

Library of Congress Cataloging in Publication Data

MacBrayne, Lewis Edward, 1872-
    One more chance.

    Reprint of the 1916 ed.
    1. Probation--Massachusetts. 2. Crime and
criminals--Massachusetts. I. Ramsay, James Petrie,
1861-   joint author. II. Title.
HV9305.M4M2 1973   364.6'3'09744   73-156023
ISBN 0-404-09124-5

Original size of this volume was 5 X 7 3/8
AMS edition is 5 X 6 7/8
Text size of this edition was reduced 5%

Foundations of Criminal Justice Series, General
Editors: Richard H. Ward and Austin Fowler, John Jay
College of Criminal Justice

Manufactured in the United States of America

TO THE MANY MEN AND
WOMEN WHO, PLEADING
FOR ONE MORE CHANCE
TO REFORM, HAVE
TURNED THEIR BACKS
UPON THE PAST AND
BECOME GOOD CITIZENS,
THIS BOOK IS SIN-
CERELY DEDICATED

CONTENTS

PREFACE

It is a curious and interesting fact that in all the centuries in which organized society has sought to protect itself against the criminal and the evil-doer, corrective punishment has been directed against his body, while his mind, until very recently, has been ignored. From the moment of the arrest of the offender, the investigation has had to do with the acts of his hands, and the sentence of incarceration or death has limited the activities of the outward man.

Classification of criminals, in like manner, depended upon the outward evidence. A man was set down as a burglar because of the patent facts that on a certain night his feet carried him to a certain building, where his hands forced an entrance and took possession of goods that did not belong to him. Since the species of burglar is an enemy to society and a constant menace, the treatment required was temporary confinement, in order to interrupt a further practice of the profession. The assumption of the law seems to have been that the race was divided into two distinct classes; organized society, upholding its own laws, and partially organized crime, lawless and seeking to prey upon its more industrious fellows.

This theory never was sound, and yet it has taken thousands of years to dispose of it. There are, it is true, the two well defined groups of law-abiding citizens and professional criminals; but there is no dead man's land between them. There is, rather, a neutral territory over which any of us may stray in a moment of weakness, discouragement or temptation; and any one of us may even touch a crime without at heart becoming what the law so long held us to be, a real criminal.

And perhaps there is no one theory in the whole history of the world that has been more thoroughly tried out than this belief that to decrease crime all those who violate the law should be punished. The museums of the old world are filled with the development of this idea. Punishment broadened and deepened until it reached its high-water mark in the ingenious and devilish tortures of the Inquisition, and in the sentence of death imposed at one time for no less than a hundred offenses that might be committed in England. Nor can we charge these "crimes against justice" to a godless age and a foreign land. One has but to turn back the pages in the history of our own New England, established in the fear of God and for the liberty of mind and conscience, to recall to what extremes we in turn were led in the mistaken zeal to stamp out crime by punishment rather than reformation.

In 1631 Philip Radcliffe was fined forty shillings, whipped, had his ears cut off and was banished for scandalous speeches against the Government and the Church at Salem. In 1652 a man was publicly whipped for being too gaily attired, and the punishment for profanity was to have the tongue bored through with a red-hot iron. Eight years later Thomas Browning was branded in the forehead with the letter "B" for burglary, and the sentence was imposed in the presence of the Court. At Worcester in 1797 Johnson Greene was executed for the same crime, and one Lindsay was branded on the hand with a hot iron for forgery. Indeed, it is hardly more than a century back to the action of the General Court that abolished the many infamous punishments that were practised in Massachusetts.

Yet neither in this country nor elsewhere in the world was crime prevented or materially lessened by the accepted method of treatment. It fluctuated back and forth in waves, and developed like a disease even in states where civilization had attained a high level, and Christianity was proclaimed from many pulpits. It imposed an increasing burden upon those who were law-abiding, until it became apparent to whoever gave serious attention to the problem that something must be wrong with the system itself. And, in truth, the system was wrong, inasmuch as it ignored the mind within the body. It failed to mark the distinction between the habitual criminal and the individual in temporary trouble with himself and the law. It took no account of the salvage to be recovered from the Courts.

II

In Bristol County in Massachusetts there stands an unique monument to the overthrow of this centuries-old theory of crime. It is a jail that cost the taxpayers $140,000, and has never been occupied, though it was authorized in 1897, and finished as speedily as stone could be laid and steel bars set in position.

In that year the prison population of Massachusetts had attained its highest point, 8173 convicted law-breakers in confinement on the thirty-first day of December, and the so-called corrective institutions of the state were becoming over-crowded. The total number committed to all penal institutions within the state that year, excepting certain industrial schools, was 31,362. Yet the granite building erected in Fall River never has held a prisoner, though the arrests made in the succeeding year were to total 99,336. For something happened in 1898 that was to reduce permanently the normal criminal population of Massachusetts to 6500, though the population of the state had increased more than a million since then, and the arrests for 1915 had reached a new mark of 179,010; even then necessitating only 26,487 commitments to penal institutions. That something was the extension of the Law of Probation.

Probation was introduced into the world,—though not put into operation as a system,—very early in the Christian era, when Christ released a woman offender against the moral law upon her own good behavior, with the admonition, "Go, and sin no more." In Massachusetts, the first state to enact this principle into law, a probation officer was authorized by Act of the General Court as early as 1878, the law, limited in its application to the City of Boston, being based upon results obtained by a volunteer probation worker. In 1891 it became mandatory upon all cities.

But probation was extended under this law only to the minor offenses that came before the lower courts, and the offenders thus released were chiefly citizens who had been arrested for drunkenness. The important act passed by the Legislature of 1898 was to check the growing prison population in that it authorized the appointment of probation officers to serve in the Superior Courts, and offered clemency, within the discretion of the judge, to prisoners charged with felonies. Such officers became virtually lay attorneys, whose attitude was friendly to the accused, and who were required to investigate the statements made by defendants in their own behalf, and determine whether there were mitigating circumstances that argued in favor of their rectitude in the future if the course of sentence was stayed. Here, for the first time, was an intelligent effort to go beyond the acts of the body and inquire into the motives of the mind. It was the beginning of a system that has since spread over the United States, and is now developing throughout the world.

Coincident with this legislation, in point of time, was another law which made radical changes in the method of dealing with criminal drunkenness, and in 1900 a further step was taken in the adoption of the French system of suspended sentences, which imposes sentence and then suspends its execution by placing the offender in the custody of a probation officer for a period of several months, at the end of which time the sentence itself expires. By this same law a better coördination of the duties of the several probation officers of the state was worked out, and a greater uniformity of administration thus secured.

In 1905 an even more radical step was taken in hehalf of the drunkard, when a law was passed providing for the release, without appearance in Court for a first or second offender within a year, the probation officer being given the power to act without the necessity of bringing the matter before the judge. Nor did this mark the end of a serious effort, on the part of earnest men and women, to reform a system that had proved inadequate to the problem of crime, for in the year following a new law was enacted with regard to delinquent and wayward children, raising the age limit at which they could be committed from 12 to 14 years, and providing court sessions apart from criminal trials. While the punitive powers of the Court have been lessened by this law, the corrective and supervisional powers have been greatly enlarged.

The frequent additions and amendments to the probation laws of Massachusetts are the strongest possible expression of the public estimate of the system and its possibilities. It bears witness to the fact that a substitute has been found for imprisonment which produces better results at far less cost.

And after an operation of this system for several years, one is able to compute the real salvage to the state; not only in dollars, but in constructive citizenship.

III

To arrive at a better understanding of this problem, let us divide serious offenses against the law into professional crime and accidental crime. This distinction is necessary, lest a too-enthusiastic follower of the theory of probation might expect from it the salvation of the state. For it is well to understand that while the professional criminal may, in rare cases, be rescued from his environment and become a good citizen again, the chances are so much against him that it has not been considered wise to offer him probation. But the occasional criminal, on the other hand, being, in the main, a weak citizen led astray, has one chance in two of a permanent rescue, and a return to the ranks of those who are law-abiding and productive. Let the point be illustrated by a case of record in Massachusetts since the passage of the laws referred to, and which is clearly defined in its application.

Two young men were returning from a dance hall in a city near Boston a few years ago, both partly under the influence of liquor and with empty pockets. They were average young men, engaged at regular occupation during the day, and with no record against them on the police blotters. Yet upon this particular night, finding themselves in front of a familiar hardware store, some impulse prompted them to enter it, and steal several revolvers and other articles that could be turned into saloon money. A few days later one of the men, while seeking to sell one of the pistols, was arrested and held for burglary. His companion of the previous night, taking alarm, left town hurriedly and was not seen thereabouts for several years.

By a quite logical reasoning it is safe to assume

that a man who burglarizes a shop in the night time and steals firearms contemplates the committing of other crimes, and public sentiment would sustain a prosecuting officer for sending him behind the bars. Yet this young man was not so sentenced. The fact that his record prior to that time had been reasonably good, and that the offense had been committed under the stimulus of liquor, gained a favorable report upon his case from the probation officer, and he was turned over to that official for an indefinite probationary period. He fulfilled this obligation for fifteen months and then went his way, his case now placed on file. Some time elapsed, and then, one day, he voluntarily called upon the probation officer for advice.

"I want to become a police officer in my town," he explained. "There are sixteen candidates for the place, and I am afraid that somebody will dig up the story of my arrest and put me out of the running. I have been an instructor of motormen for one of the large street railway companies since I last saw you, and I have kept the pledge that I took, but this old trouble may stand in my way. What shall I do?"

"Go to the selectmen and tell them the story yourself," advised the officer of the Court.

The young man did so; and this act of frankness decided the appointment in his favor. He not only became a police officer, but he is today one of the best in the state. He has made a specialty of liquor prosecutions, and there is hardly a term of the Superior Court when he does not appear to follow up his cases. In other words, probation not only kept him from crime, but it made a constructive citizen out of him.

But the illustration does not end here. His companion on the night of that early indiscretion, because his recklessness was not checked at the time, became first an occasional criminal, and finally a professional. In one of his attempted robberies he shot a police officer, was tried for attempted murder, and is now serving a life sentence at the expense of the tax-payers.

In that case you have the definition of accidental and professional crime. The first man may properly be termed the salvage of state; but the second was not reached in time, and so became social wreckage, beyond redemption.

The generally accepted classification of criminals places them in one of three groups; those who are born or are instinctive criminals, those who are professional criminals by acquired habits, and the single offenders. Investigations made in the Massachusetts Reformatory have established the fact that about one in every six of the inmates is feeble-minded, or sub-normal; and it may be said in passing that it yet remains to segregate these unfortunates in special corrective institutions. They cannot be counted as good material for spiritual regeneration.

In the second group is the pickpocket who has graduated from petty thieving, the flat-worker, the yegg whose specialty is the bank or the postoffice, the armed house burglar, the highwayman, the counterfeiter, the forger; and others who have specialized in crime. Did these two groups constitute the majority of the persons arrested for committing crime, and the single offender typify only the occasional recruit to the ranks of those who are forever hunted by the police, probation might appear to the cynical to be more of a theory than a practical, self-justifying fact. But the reverse is the truth.

Of the 179,010 persons arrested in Massachusetts in 1915, for example, all of whom would have obtained court records under the old law, 50,336 were automatically released for simple drunkenness, many never to return again because of the fear of public disgrace so narrowly averted. It is idle, perhaps, to seek to estimate this salvage in dollars, since one cannot determine how many of them would have suffered temporary loss of employment through detention, or through loss of self respect have begun to slip down the social scale more readily. But it is a conservative estimate to assume that such loss, had the probationers been taken into the open Court and fined, with an absence from at least one day's occupation, would have averaged

$5 for each person involved, and this totals over $250,000.

But the larger item of salvage is to be found in the 126,559 prisoners held for trial. Of these several thousand came within the scope of the probation officer's service, and a certain proportion of them were likewise given a chance to return to an honest life. What was the actual saving here? Obviously it is not to be found in multiplying the number released on probation by an average weekly wage, though this would easily produce a total of from a half to three quarters of a million dollars. There is a simpler and more authoritative method.

We have the records of one Massachusetts Superior Court probation officer who has served for fourteen years, and who has had 3000 cases under his personal charge within that period, keeping complete records in every instance, which are now available for analysis. Of this number 55 per cent. have been permanently saved, and have remained good citizens. Another 10 per cent. have earned a fair rating. They have kept within the law, but have not become constructive citizens as did the potential burglar who is now a police officer, or as did others whose stories will be related in the pages that follow. This leaves 35 per cent. of the 3000; and it may be stated that they have degenerated into various types, from weak citizens to vagabonds and professional criminals.

Yet the record, citing only this single court in one county of the state, is a splendid one. As a business proposition it is sound and profitable. It represents the salvage of society of which we have spoken; the souls, reputations, careers of usefulness that otherwise might have been lost.

IV

After all, abstract reasoning is interesting only to the student of special problems. The tax-payer who is asked to support reforms requires that they be translated into items of human interest.

The purpose of the narrative that follows is to examine a number of these real cases, seeking to point out the paths that led to crime, the methods by which the progress of those who walked in them was arrested and the ultimate return to the service of the state—for we all serve the state who obey its laws—of those whose feet have strayed. They are genuine human documents, the names used alone being fictitious, related as faithfully as the incidents can be recalled, and not colored for the purpose of obtaining more dramatic effects. And indeed there is no need for fiction here, since human fact is intensely dramatic or pathetic when it runs at cross purposes to the main currents of our established life. One has but to serve these people with sympathy and honesty to come face to face with their personal problems, and discover the impulses that have urged them on.

It only remains, in this prefatory chapter, to speak a word concerning the joint authorship of the book. The experiences in the pages that follow are those of Mr. James P. Ramsay, a probation officer in Massachusetts since the law was extended to apply to cases before the Superior Court, and one who has been a factor in obtaining important amendments to it, and who has inspired the adoption of a somewhat similar law now applying to the whole of Scotland. Certain of these experiences I have shared with him as a private investigator of this highly important experiment in human salvage. All of his data, voluminously gathered, has been at my disposal for examination and classification. To give proper strength to the narratives, it has seemed best to report them all in the first person; and a collaboration has permitted this to be done from a surer perspective, and with a more impartial eye to dramatic values. The personality of the man in this case looms large, it may be admitted, yet the work of the probation officers in other counties than Middlesex and other states than Massachusetts has been almost uniformly successful, and the variety of their experiences quite as interesting. What is true in this historic county is to be duplicated elsewhere: the probation officer has become a lay lawyer for the poor and those in distress quite beyond the province of the duties originally assigned to him. To his door at night come many people upon strange errands: the clergyman, seeking advice in solving the unexpected problem that has come up in his own parish; the man of wealth, begging that an intemperate son be saved for the fortune that he must eventually administer; the brilliant young fellow, confessing that he has become a dope fiend, and seeking some remedy; the young girl, facing discovery and disgrace, and fearing the anger of her own people.

One cannot know these facts, gained from an intimate observation of the work of such an officer, and from the close reading of the hundreds of confessions on file in his study, without feeling deeply that here is a story that ought to be told; not only because of its intense human interest, but also as a document of record in behalf of those who have been saved by the overthrow of a system older than civilization.

L. E. M.

A Classic on Probation Revisited

A Preface to the New Edition of
ONE MORE CHANCE

In 1898 the Law of Probation was passed by the Massachusetts State Legislature. This extended the 1878 Probation Act which had been limited only to the city of Boston and the amended Act of 1891 which extended the Act to all Massachusetts cities. The crucialness of the 1898 Act was the authorization of probation officers to serve in the Superior Courts and thereby extend the clemency and compassion of probation, from its limited drunkeness violators, to prisoners charged with felonies. Thus it was that justice ceased being "blind" and was given "eyes" to see beyond the offense, to the offender.

Central to this legislation was the creation of the probation officer function. The function consisted of the investigation of the defendent's statement as well as an evaluation of mitigating circumstances and the defendent's attitude and projection of rehabilitative chances if granted the staying of sentencing. Additionally, the probation officer was charged with maintaining — and chosen for — the empathy and objectivity required to evaluate the person behind a crime.

Probation in Massachusetts was granted the French system of suspended sentences in 1900, which imposed sentencing and then suspended execution by placing the offender in the custody of a probation officer for the sentence period. While this law was focused initially on crimes of drunkeness, its extension to other crimes followed soon after. In 1905, again in behalf of the drunkard, a law was passed providing for the release, without appearance in court, for a first or second offender within a year; this allowed the probation officer the power to act without bringing the offender to court. One year later, in an attempt to deal more equitable with juvenile crime, the Massachusetts legislature raised the age limit of commitment on juvenile delinquents and wayward children from 12 to 14 years and provided for court sessions separate from criminal trials.

The key element to the probation system lies beyond the very real monetary advantages of supervised release as opposed to incarceration; it is, more importantly, found in the retention of a person's worth and reinstitution of self confidence. It provided for reappraisal by giving them a second chance at respect and freedom.

MacBrayne and Ramsay are quick to point out that probation, as they view it, is not a way of dealing with the professional criminal. They are aware that the professional is constantly manipulating his environment for the greatest possible reward and smallest possible punishment. Their population is the tempted, impulsive, weak, and easily-led occasional criminal who, fearing the very real debilitating effects of incarceration, is, in effect, a "better bet" for probation's clemency.

The case is further made by MacBrayne and Ramsay that there is a "timeliness" to probation, citing the example of two young men who engaged in an impulsive burglary. The youth who got caught was justly repentent and used the probation period to consider the consequences of his act. The young man who got away considered crime so easy and profitable that he soon entered the ranks of the professionals. Probation for the latter youth after several "uncaught" crimes would not serve the same function as that of the initial offense clemency. As an epilogue, it is pointed out that this latter youth eventually "graduated" to armed robbery and in one of his attempts shot a police officer and served a life sentence at considerable taxpayer expense. In this one example can be seen the MacBrayne and Ramsay premise of human wreckage as opposed to human salvage.

A question worth asking is how successful has the experiment in human salvage really been? The answer is partially provided in the more than 3000 cases analysed and faithfully recorded by a probation officer in the Massachusetts Superior Court with fourteen years of service. The perusal of his records revealed that 55 per cent of his probationers were leading productive and useful lives. Another 10 per cent, while not as outstanding by measurement of income, family status or worldly goods, had marginally adjusted and had not subsequently run afoul of the law. The remaining 35 per cent ran the gamut from vagabond to professional criminal. The point to make here is that a success rate of 65 percent is seldom claimed in any scientific discipline let alone in the tricky area of human behavior outcome. In contrast is the percentile of recidivism in the incarceration statistics which predict return of offenders to upwards of 75 per cent.

The case is then made for a dollar-and-cent analysis that would show that the cost of probation services is well below that of incarceration upkeep and, more importantly, provides a return in the constructive activities of these benefactors of "one more chance."

The special lure of this book, published some 56 years ago, is not in its recitation of probation's early history, or in its statistical presentation of the system's justification. The lure is in the focus of the real people who ran afoul of the law and through probation — while not always entirely readusted — were given the remnants of respect and productivity in a way that no "eye for eye" system could ever begin to provide.

My search for the most poignant description of what these pages contain began and ended in the words written by MacBrayne in *One More Chance*:

"The documents are genuine human documents, the names alone being fictitious, related as faithfully as the incidents can be recalled, and not colored for the purpose of obtaining more dramatic effects. And indeed there is no need for fiction here, since human fact is intensely dramatic or pathetic when it runs to cross purposes to the main current of our established life. One has but to serve these people with sympathy and honesty to come face to face with their personal problems, and discover the impulses that have urged them on."

Given the 1972 reality of identity crises, covert and overt oppression, increasing alienation and cancerous depression and apathy, it may be that the cases chronicled herein appear dated by time and place, but their truth and universal timeliness are apparent from beginning to end.

This probation "classic" was jointly authored by James P. Ramsay and Lewis E. MacBrayne. Ramsay, a probation officer in the State of Massachusetts was a man known for the emapthy and objectivity previously mentioned in the preface and considered today to have been one of the pioneering voices in this system for human reclamation. Lewis E. MacBrayne was the writing arm of the team; he pictured himself as faithful collaborater and structural presentor of the cases which are reported out in the first person narrative for a still interesting literary "you are there" style.

H. Bruce Pierce
John Jay College
of Criminal Justice
New York, N.Y.

ONE MORE CHANCE

CHAPTER I

MY FIRST DAY AS A PROBATION OFFICER

I really saw the great machinery of the Massachusetts Courts in motion for the first time on a sunny day late in September, in the year 1901. It was not my first day in a Court—for that matter, I had even served as a juryman,—but there is a difference between the point of view of the casual spectator, or the juror, and that of one in the position in which I now found myself. For I had become a probation officer under the new state law; an officer of the Court who was to stand, henceforth, between certain prisoners at the bar, and the sentence that might be awaiting them.

It was the opening of the fall term of the Criminal Court, and the docket was unusually heavy. The district attorney was nearing the end of his term of service, and had expressed a desire to dispose of all pending cases. I sat there in my newly acquired seat, and hour after hour the wheels of justice were speeded up until, before the end of the afternoon session, nearly a hundred men and

women had faced the bench. I have no doubt that
the spectators who crowded the public seats derived
a certain amount of entertainment at these quick
pleas of "Guilty" and "Not guilty," with the sudden bursts of pleading or passion that were to be
heard from time to time; but on that day I looked
beneath the skin, as it were, in my earnest desire to
discern the human being within the body.

I noted, as I had never done before, the manner
in which the prisoners received the sentences imposed upon them; the indifferent or contemptuous
smiles; the stolid look meant for bravado; the mut-
tered curse or suppressed cry of anger; the clenched
hands and the faces blanched in despair. There
were young men in their teens, already blighted for
life; men in middle life, hardened and debauched;
men with grey hair, the pathetic victims of alcohol;
girls upon the threshold of life, fallen and degraded.

And then it came over me, all at once, that I had
lightly accepted a position of responsibility so grave
that all of my experience in life must fail before it.
Who was I, after all, to undertake the duties and
powers imposed upon me! Every new probation
officer, I surmise, feels the weight of these obliga-
tions, but to me they were already sitting in judgment upon my qualifications. I began to run over
in my mind the list of things that I was expected
to do. I must consider whether the offender had
made a full and free confession of guilt; whether

he would work and provide for his dependents; whether his statement of name, residence and age was true; whether he was more the victim of circumstances than the product of criminal instinct.

Suddenly the court room became very still, and the deliberate, even voice of the judge focussed public attention upon me: "Mr. Probation Officer, have you looked into this case, and have you any recommendation to make in behalf of the prisoner at the bar?"

I looked up startled, and beheld my first case. The prisoner at the bar was a young man, well dressed, clean looking, with no signs of viciousness about him. I had not observed him up to that moment, and in my preoccupation I had not heard the charge to which he had just pleaded. I forced myself to reply to the judge that I was unacquainted with his history, and would like time to investigate. The case was at once continued, and the defendant was led away to my new probation office.

"What was the charge?" I inquired in a low voice of the officer in charge of the case.

"Burglary, and he tried to kill a police officer," was the reply.

We sat down in the clean, sunny room, the burglar and I, and faced each other. Disrobed of the circumstances that brought us there, we were probably two fellow men, liable to errors of judgment, endowed with more or less common sense, and neither marked for success nor failure by our birth. If I could get beyond the fact that now clothed him as a prisoner and a desperate character, I might find the man who had gone astray. If he should pierce my own official disguise, he would discover a man who had begun his life work in the coal mines as a child of ten, who had become messenger and telegraph operator at twelve, who had fired a locomotive at fifteen and been in charge of a switch tower at sixteen, who had emigrated to the United States at eighteen and opened the first switch tower in America, who in later years had been well enough thought of by his fellow men to serve as a member of the Massachusetts Legislature, and who had now come into the present responsibility.

"Well," said I, "tell me all about it."

"What?" he asked doubtfully.

"Tell me the whole story. Perhaps I can help you."

He did so. It seemed to me then a vivid, unusually human story, but the experience of later years has duplicated it many times.

He was born in Massachusetts, and his parents were respectable people, who planned for him a high school education. "I began to go wrong when I was in the grammar school," he told me. "There was a group of older boys in our village, who hung out on the streets at night, and who seemed to have a better time than the boys who were required to remain at home. I aspired to become a member of this gang, and to stand well in its favor, and my parents had so much confidence in me that they did not question my whereabouts when I began to come in during the evening. I learned to smoke, and at the high school age, took an occasional drink. By the time I had gone to work, I had been initiated into the exciting game of poker, and was ready to risk money that I was now earning. I was an easy mark for the older boys, but they had admitted me to full fellowship in the gang, and I thought that I was getting my money's worth in experience: but before long I was losing more money each week than I earned. Then I began to borrow. I thought that I could win back what I had lost, but I had no such luck. A time came when nobody would loan me money, and I was hard pushed to pay what I owed."

It was at this point that his criminal career began. False environment had created an abnormal need, and temptation was soon beckoning a finger at him. The post-office was in the village general store, and calling there one afternoon to ask for the family mail, he found the place quite deserted for the moment, and slipped around and took a look into the cash register. The sum of its contents was not large, but he helped himself, and escaped detection. Petty thieving is not so difficult when suspicion does not fasten itself upon you. He called again and again; until finally the proprietor never left the place unguarded for a moment.

The money had now become necessary to the thief, but the opportunity was no longer a matter of chance. This fact irritated him for a time, and then he planned a midnight visit to the store. He went armed with a revolver, not because he considered himself a professional burglar, but for self protection!

"I was familiar with every foot of the place," he said, "and I made almost no noise in getting in, yet before I could reach the cash register a voice in the darkness cried, 'Hands up.' I did not reply, but I drew my pistol and fired in the direction of the voice. An answering shot came back, and it was only luck that neither one of us was hit. I was frightened now, and anxious only to make my escape. I ran out by the way I had come, and my first plan was to go to the barn of a neighbor who had a good saddle horse, make a dash across the country, and perhaps gain money for my escape by holding somebody up. Yet I gave this idea up almost instantly, and ran home instead. We had a summer house fitted up for a sleeping porch, and I threw off my clothes and got into bed. I had the feeling that they would come for me, and they did. I had fired at one of the town police, and the shots had awakened a citizen who saw me running down the street. They did not believe me when I said that I had been in bed all night, and so I was arrested, and have been in jail for several weeks. I have spent many sleepless nights thinking over what a fool I have been."

So that was my first case! I tried to consider whether it came within the list of those to which the law desired to extend clemency. What mitigating circumstance could I find? The young man on his own confession had gone from the petty vices of gambling and thieving to armed burglary, and had his aim been true might now be facing trial for murder. Yet the judge had asked my opinion in the case, and that seemed to assume that perhaps there might be a chance to save the youth.

I began to probe deeper into his home environment, and after a time I brought to light an interesting fact. The parents were not of the same religious faith, and they had not been able to agree as to whether he should be brought up a Protestant or a Catholic. Consequently he had been without spiritual training, and therefore without moral responsibility. It was my own observation in life that a man without the fear of God somewhere in his heart was sailing his craft without a rudder, and was playing in luck if he did not bring up on a reef sooner or later. So I decided to make the first use of my prerogative and give the prisoner at the bar the benefit of the doubt.

The judge accepted my recommendation, though

he had settled in his own mind, as I learned later, on a term of imprisonment of from two to three years. I think that I took the case with some trembling, but the months passed with the young man industriously working, and in due time the case was placed on file and forgotten.

That was fourteen years ago, and one summer evening recently I found myself thinking of him, and set out to look him up, if he was still to be found. It was a less difficult matter than I had imagined, but when I stood face to face with him in the pleasant home to which I had been directed, neither of us recognized the other for a moment. He was married and had three fine children; and the wife knew his story, and had stood by him loyally. He was earning a comfortable living for them, and was respected by his neighbors.

My mind went back to that September afternoon when I had seen so much misery and crime, and had been given the opportunity to say whether this man should step out of the line, or continue on with the others to prison; and I looked about me at his home, and at his children, and I said to myself: "This is the salvage of state. We might have broken this man, and, instead, we saved him. The process doesn't even stop here, but goes on through the lives of his three children."

What will the spiritual training of that family be? Well, I know this much. He gave me the

code that he wrote out years before, during his
probationary supervision, as a guide to other young
men, and it is this: "Keep good company. Keep
good hours. Keep an open ear to your parents'
advice. Be honest and speak the truth." Look
back on his own youth as I have related it, and you
will see that this statement covers all the points
upon which he went astray, and adds one more for
himself as a parent. I will trust the future of his
boys and girls.

What I gained from that first case, perhaps above
any other experience, was an understanding of the
fact that no offender can be recommended for probation merely because of an appeal to one's sym
pathy. There must be some definite reason for
giving the man his one more chance, and from that
day to this I have never failed to seek it. Some
judges require me to prove my reason for setting
aside the sentence of the lower court; and this is
reasonable, and a fair basis for a recommendation.

In a study of several thousand cases since that
first day in court I have also come to recognize the
occasional offender from the professional criminal,
and I realize how hopeless reform is in the case of
the latter. For the professional criminal, far from
being penitent, takes a certain boastful pride in his
work that survives arrest and subsequent conviction. I do not mean that such a criminal never
tires of his profession and honestly desires to wipe

out his past, but I do affirm that nine times out of ten when a burglar or a yegg is apprehended, his first inquiry to me is likely to be as to what judge will sit upon his case; and, if he does not happen to know him, what his reputation is for severity. As a rule, they know all about the judges in the state where they are operating, and can discuss their personal traits, and the nature of an appeal that is most likely to influence them. It is a part of their trade to keep posted in such matters, just as it is to have an inside knowledge of the institutions to which they may be sent.

There is a fugitive from justice at the present time known under the name of Chesterfield, a flat worker who has operated in many cities, and who upon more than one occasion has been in the toils of the police. I have talked with him many times, but it never occurred to me to recommend him for probation, nor did he seek my assistance for such a purpose. His business is that of entering houses while the lawful occupants are absent, for the purpose of abstracting any jewelry or money that they may have left behind, and when the misfortune of his calling lands him behind the bars, he at once devotes all of his mental energies to the problem of getting out.

Upon the last occasion when I talked with him, he had been sentenced to prison, but he privately assured me that he did not intend long to remain there. His first step was to feign insanity, and he did it so well that he was sent to another institution for treatment. While there he made an impression of a keyhole with a piece of soap, and with this for a model constructed a key from a piece of bone, and so made his escape. If ever I come across him again, I shall expect that he will relate the details of this adventure as a tribute to his professional cleverness, rather than ask me to intercede for him that he may lead a better life.

There is a professional traveler of my acquaintance who sometimes sits down with me for an evening, and over his cigar relates the methods by which he extracts orders from unwilling buyers. There is no by-path of the business that he has not explored, not a contingency that he has not anticipated. Should the Statutes be suddenly amended, making the business of a traveling salesman a misdemeanor, I don't suppose that this man would be able to give up his occupation.

Sometimes I think that such men as Chesterfield have fooled themselves into believing that stealing is a real profession, and that it is a mistaken public idea that has brought about the restrictions imposed by the law and the police.

"When my two partners and myself are planning to start out on a new trip," he said to me one day, "we go to our tailor in New York and get fitted out with the season's clothes, not flashy, but respectable. We try to make up as successful business men. Then we take down a map of New England and select a route of cities. Arrived in one of them, we take a bird's-eye view of the town and select the residential quarter where we want to do business. We seldom work more than two hours a day; and this is one of the pleasant things about the profession: you have a lot of time for your own amusement.

"We start in at about two o'clock, when Susie has gone to school for the afternoon, and mother has started out to shop or make her calls. One man remains in the street to keep a sharp lookout for the police or anybody returning to the house. We ring the doorbell, and if anybody responds, merely inquire for a fictitious person supposed to live upon that street. If nobody comes, we ring again. Then we make a quick search for the key that mother often leaves on the outside for Susie. As there are only two or three such hiding places, we soon discover whether it is there; and if it is not, we enter the house by a skeleton key. Our first move on the inside is to go swiftly to the back door and unlock it, ready for a hurried exit. Our second is to look into all the chambers to see whether anybody is lying down. We search only the bureau drawers as a rule, and if any valuables are there, they are frequently to be found in the two top ones, which occasionally are locked. But the locks never bother us any.   They can be forced, and in a few moments we are ready to depart and try our luck in another house.   It is safe and easy work!"

There is no hint of reform in such a confession as that.   I have broached the subject to Chesterfield, but it never appeared to interest him.   He never told me the story of how he started in crime, and I have observed the same reticence on the part of other professionals with whom I have talked. Men seldom tell about their downfall until there is repentance, and you cannot help them until this comes about.   A man's brain or his glib tongue is not his conscience, and until you can find the latter you have not located the man himself.

CHAPTER II

IMAGINATION AS A FACTOR IN CRIME

The deeper one goes into the investigation of crime, the more profoundly one is impressed with the variety of causes that lead young men and women to commit misdemeanors. Psychologists have certain definite groups to which they assign all malefactors, but a study of the individual case often locates the impulse to wrong-doing in an unexpected quarter. Let me illustrate this by the recital of two cases in which imagination was the factor in crime.

There came into my office one afternoon a frankly distressed police inspector and a well dressed, modest appearing girl of sixteen. There is a human side to these detectives, as they are more popularly known, that is not always shown to the public, for they take quite as much pride in their profession as does the criminal whom they so often hunt. There is a saying within the prisons that "when a first class 'bull' gets down on you, he won't stop at anything to send you up," and quite likely this has been true in certain states where a police officer's experience with professional thugs is not always of a pleasant nature, and where the absence of evidence, in a case where guilt is reasonable to assume, has prompted a frame-up of some sort rather than permit a dangerous criminal to evade the law.

But this inspector was not of that class.   He had made an arrest very much desired at headquarters, and yet it troubled him.   "See what you can do with this case," he said to me.   "It seems a pity to give the girl the publicity of the Courts."

"What is the charge?" I inquired.

"This is the girl who robbed the letter boxes two years ago," he answered.   "You may remember that there was some stir about it at the time, for she took letters containing checks and then cashed them on forged signatures.   We recognized her upon the street today and brought her in, and she confesses to seven counts.   But she seems to have been a good girl for the past two years, and perhaps you had better look into the matter."

I turned to this demure, innocent appearing girl in amazement.   Not only had the police of a large city tried in vain to apprehend her in 1910, but the Federal authorities had put picked men upon her trail without success.   She had operated so successfully, under their very noses, and had disappeared with such ease when they tried to close in upon her, that the only conclusion was that she had some powerful gang behind her, the more dangerous because it kept under cover.

Now and then there is a young woman so clever in her character pose that even a police inspector of mature experience is deceived, and it occurred to me that perhaps here was such an actress, who was relying on us to gain her way to freedom. I closed the door and invited her to sit down, and prepared myself for an adroit appeal to my sympathy.

It did not come; at least not in the manner that I had anticipated. She confessed to having obtained $169 by stealing letters from mail boxes, but was so conscientious in answering all the questions put to her that finally I interrupted to ask: "But why did you do it?"

She hung her head for a moment, as though ashamed of herself, and then confessed: "I was a great reader at the age of twelve to fourteen, and my favorite books were detective stories. I used to think them over and plan crimes for myself, and then I tried one to see if I could not do it without being caught by the real detectives. I was successful, again and again, and it seemed very exciting."

After I had made a careful inquiry into the history of this girl, I was able to construct her story. At fourteen she was pretty, self-possessed, and had acquired some local reputation as an elocutionist. The very nature of this circumstance taught her to act other parts than her own, and also created a need for pretty dresses. Her mother was in rather poor circumstances, and could not afford to meet the demand for her public appearances, though it did not appear that the daughter ever complained of this fact. The money that she obtained, however, was used to purchase dresses and other finery.

Even now I wonder at the resources of a girl, only just beyond the grammar school age, that permitted her to act with such a knowledge of business affairs. She made a study of seven prominent families, learned when checks were sent to them in payment of rent or other business transactions, and not only purloined the letters undetected, but endorsed the checks and used them.

Upon one occasion she bought a dress at a store on Winter Street in Boston, the purchase amounting to $16.50, and so well did she conduct herself that when she offered a check $8.50 in excess of that sum, there was no hesitation in giving her the balance in money. Nor was she satisfied to obtain the money by the easiest methods, but constantly sought new adventures.

One of her victims was a well known lawyer; a fact that may have spurred her on to special effort. He had received a check for $75, and when she gained possession of this, she conceived a plan to pass herself off as his daughter. So she wrote to a leading Boston firm, stating that she was going abroad on short notice, and ordering sent to her a pink chiffon evening dress, a broadcloth opera coat, patent leather boots, silk stockings, a sailor suit and a red silk tie. "I enclose check," she wrote, "and if it is not sufficient I will mail another covering the balance. If it is too much, please send me the difference in cash with the goods."

On the following day she called the firm up on the telephone, stated that she had given an order by mail, and inquired as to the hour of the probable delivery. It was necessary to prevent the goods reaching the inside of the lawyer's home. This information obtained, she went to the street in question, and as she saw the delivery wagon approaching, took her place on the steps of the residence, as though just leaving the house. Imagine such audacity in a child!

Yet her plan worked without a flaw. She met the parcel clerk, inquired for her goods, signed for them, and learned that they came to the full amount of the check.

After a time she wearied of the game, or may have discovered that the police were working closer to her trail, as indeed they were. One day she asked permission of her mother to visit relatives in Nova Scotia, and arrayed in her dishonestly acquired finery she slipped away, and did not return for two years.

But she came back mature, reticent and desirous of working for her living. She secured employment with a reputable firm, and when arrested was earning $14 a week, and saw disaster staring her in the face if the charges against her were pressed. One can easily ruin a girl of sixteen, and this one seemed to be so genuinely penitent that the Court gave her the opportunity, on my recommendation, to make restitution at the rate of $5 a week through the probation officer. She accepted and was placed on probation, and the story did not get into the newspapers. In less than a year she had paid back the $169, and since then, so far as I know, she has been traveling the straight and narrow way, with every promise of making a good woman.

Would justice have been served better by a trial and imprisonment? Restitution would not have been possible in that case, the girl would have ceased to be a productive wage-earner, and most important of all, she would have been branded a criminal, to be returned to the world in due season broken in spirit or graduated into real crime, where her cleverness might have made her an adept.

The second case in which an appeal to the imagination was an incentive to crime, is one well worthy of the study of any psychologist. John Black was a boy who read with the keenest delight the detective stories of A. Conan Doyle and Gaboriau. There was never a "Sherlock Holmes" story written that he did not read, and like all normal youths, he was on the side of the famous investigator rather than that of the criminals whose mysteries he solved.

"Indeed, I would have preferred being shot to committing any of the crimes of which I read," he told me later. "But the subject had a tremendous fascination for me, and I saw in it a great imaginative field for the writer."

At the age of sixteen young Black decided that he would become a story writer, and that Sir Arthur Conan Doyle should be his standard. In fact, he did write several detective stories during this period, though none was ever published; an experience not uncommon to youthful writers. At seventeen he abandoned fiction for more remunerative fact, and found employment in a corporation counting-room, where he did so well that his pay was raised at the end of a year. Six months later, however, found him out of employment, due to business conditions.

He seems to have worried a great deal over this, until finally he became critically ill; and when he had become convalescent a bladder ailment developed, which left him mentally depressed, and not too sure of himself. He sought work in a half-hearted way, apprehensive that he would not find it, and not disappointed in this respect, at least. Finally he decided to take his own life and end it all.

If there is any truth in the statement that it requires courage to become a suicide, this young man was no coward, for he attempted it no less than three times without success. He took chloroform once and morphine twice, but because he did not understand the nature of these drugs, survived, more wretched and disheartened than ever. Fate seemed determined to keep him upon the earth, but to do nothing else for him. How miserable he really was at this time his own parents did not suspect, for he kept the knowledge from them, taking all the blame for his failure upon himself.

Then, one day, E. W. Horning's "Amateur Cracksman" came into his hands. He read it fascinated. It seemed a direct appeal to him. In the opening chapter he saw himself in Bunny who, financially ruined, and with no help in sight, attempts suicide in the presence of Raffles, whose identity as a notorious cracksman he does not know.

The latter takes the pistol from him, you may recall, and a moment later Bunny says:

"I was a desperate man when I came in here. I'm just as desperate now. I don't mind what I do, if only I can get out of this without a scandal."

"I wonder if you mean all that?" says Raffles at length. "You do in your present mood; but who can back his moods to last?"

"I've made such a mess of my own affairs that I trust myself about as little as I'm likely to be trusted by anybody else," Bunny answers.

Raffles leads him on in this mood. "Yet you would stop at nothing for a pal?" he observes.

"At nothing in this world."

"Not even at a crime?" says Raffles, smiling.

"No, not even at that."

Raffles commits him that night to partnership in the robbery of a jeweler's shop, and they come away with their pockets loaded with loot. Bunny is fascinated and horrified by turns at the adventure, but finally declares: "I can't go back on what I have done. I wouldn't if I could. I've gone to the devil anyhow."

That was what John Black, in his mentally weakened state, read. The ingenious, cynical appeal of the apparently respectable Raffles got him as though the amateur cracksman had been in the room talking to him. For Raffles argued that a man should not steal unless sore pressed, and that once he made a good coup, he should chuck the business for all time.

"I did not plan to turn professional crook," said Black to me, recounting his emotions at this time. "I made up my mind that I would enter a shop somewhere and secure enough money to keep me going until I could finish my studies. I had belonged to a night class in stenography and I wanted to go on with it. I thought I saw a way to better myself, and then make quiet restitution for what I had stolen."

But he did not commit the crime that night, as Bunny did in the story. For two whole months he argued the matter over with himself, pro and con, sometimes shrinking from it, and again convincing himself that he only intended to exact a loan from the world, to be paid back in his own time. A man is his own enemy at such a crisis, because he is taking his own judgment as to the wisdom of his own course. At the end of two months Black had decided to turn cracksman; "for I was then past the time of sane judgment, and could not look at things in a reasonable light," he said.

Raffles and Bunny, you may remember, came from their first venture with enough plunder to pay their debts and live respectably for several months. But Black had no Raffles with him, and did not meet with any such luck. He entered a store by smashing a glass pane in the rear, located the till, forced it open—and secured 40 cents in coppers! Disgusted, he turned his attention to the grocery store next door, prowled about until he found the money drawer, took all the money that it contained—and so obtained 6 cents more. He had become a criminal, had twice risked discovery and arrest, and his reward was less than a plumber could earn in the same length of time.

He returned home sick at heart over the whole sorry business, with a full realization of what he had done, and a contempt for what it had netted him. Robbery in fiction and robbery in fact were not the same profession, apparently; a discovery that might have provided him material for a real story had he been in the mood to apply it.

Yet the fascination of the adventure returned to him, and a few nights later he started out to rob a coal office, where he had reason to believe a considerable sum of money might be found in the safe. The finger of fate, in the form of an approaching patrolman, warned him, and he fled from the contemplated crime.

He now resolved to abandon the profession definitely; and yet when he read, a few days later, of the robbery of a Boston and Maine Railroad station, he thought at once of a town where a similar break could be made, and he went there, forcing an entrance without much difficulty.

It had not occurred to him that there would be a safe here instead of a till, and so he was forced to content himself with mileage books and trip tickets, also carrying away the station stamp to use on them. But here again he found himself only a sorry amateur, for he had forgotten the dating punch, and it was necessary to return a few nights after this to secure it. While he was about it, he robbed another station further down the line, and increased his supply of mileage.

His career ended soon after. He sought to dispose of several tickets with a pawnbroker, was arrested by an inspector who anticipated that the thief would do this very thing, and promptly confessed and returned all of the property that he had stolen.

There was a division of opinion among the court

officers as to whether this young man should be placed upon probation, or sentenced as an example to others. Hardly a month passes in Massachusetts without the robbery of some suburban railroad office, and arrests are so infrequent that public sentiment calls for summary action when a thief is in the toils. Yet John Black was truly penitent, and had restored $650 in property taken in two burglaries.

I turned the case over in my mind, wondering whether it offered a chance of salvage, or whether the youth, not yet twenty years old, was too much of a wreck to be worth bothering with. He had committed four distinct breaks, and had acted deliberately in his downward course, being quite capable of making the distinction between right and wrong. Was there any safe presumption that stress of circumstances might not lead him into crime again?

Looking into his environment and antecedents, I discovered that he had been one of a large family burdened with poverty, and that his early years had been spent with his grandmother. He had never known a father's advice, and while obedient and honest, and of excellent habits, had been left too much to his own companionship, and had gone to work early in order to escape being a burden on others.

When the case finally came before the Court for disposal, an uncle by marriage appeared and offered to take him into his home if released, and the kindly president of the railroad, to whom a direct appeal had been made by this man, asked that he be placed on probation.

John Black seemed to have reached the turn in the lane at last, and three days after he had gone out a free man he had secured work, and wrote me that he would walk uprightly in the future, and would give his friends no more cause for trouble. I rather anticipated an interesting outcome of this case; but I was destined to disappointment. My next news of him recorded his death. Remorse had overwhelmed him, and in the hour when his discouragements seemed at an end, he took morphine and died a suicide.

Possibly a psychologist would deduce from a study of the facts as I have related them that the return of the suicide impulse indicated that even had he lived he must have reverted to crime eventually; that these two impulses were the chief ones with which he had to contend in his morbid nature. Possibly he feared this sinister influence, and chose what seemed to him the lesser of two evils. But could we have saved him by the old method of imprisonment, which must have fed the very mental depression from which he suffered? I do not believe so.

The State said to him: "You have one more chance to make good. It is up to you."

But like Bunny in the story, he replied: "I've made such a mess of my own affairs that I trust myself about as little as I'm likely to be trusted by anybody else."

CHAPTER III

THE PROBLEM OF THE RICH MAN'S SON

There are many people in the world ready to assign poverty as the cause of the crime that seems to breed in the slums, but I do not remember to have heard anybody proclaim riches as an equal source of law-breaking. We are prone to assume that because men steal and defraud to obtain the money that they need, the possession of wealth must remove the primary cause of wrong-doing. But such a conclusion ignores the old adage that money is the root of all evil; not only among those who desire it, but also among those who possess it.

In my own classification, based upon the experience of many years, I have come to recognize wealth as a possible, thought infrequent, source of crime, and it follows that its treatment calls for a special consideration. Probation alone is not sufficient to reform the young blood whose career has exceeded the social speed limit, and who has been brought to book by an officer of the law. Let me illustrate this point with the story that follows.

Two burglaries had been committed in a Massachusetts city that rather prided itself on the suppression of such crime, and the police were alert to guard against further breaks when word came hurriedly to headquarters that a patrolman had discovered the crooks at work, and that they were still within the building. Armed officers were hurried to the scene, and as the burglars sought to escape they were taken at the point of the revolver. They proved to be two well dressed young fellows nineteen years of age, and when they were questioned at headquarters as to their identity, one of them gave an exclusive private school for boys as his place of residence.

The police, somewhat skeptical, followed this clue, and were rewarded by finding in a waste basket, and thrown carelessly about the room, loot that had been obtained in the earlier breaks. The arrests at once assumed considerable importance.

Contrary to popular belief, the rich man's son is not always released as soon as his identity becomes known, and this precious pair found themselves held under heavy bonds for the Grand Jury. Whereupon a respectable old gentleman who controlled a chain of twenty-six stores in as many cities appeared upon the scene with three lawyers, one of them so important that he required a retaining fee of a thousand dollars, and when the case came to trial,—an indictment having been duly returned,—there was a legal battle to obtain the liberation of the prisoners.

It is a question whether this array of legal talent would have availed against the unbroken testimony of the police witnesses, had not a discriminating judge, looking beyond the evidence, sensed some special motive behind the crime, and hesitated at sending the youths to a penal institution. The case was referred to the probation officer for an investigation and report, and I began an inquiry that was destined to commit me to an interesting experiment.

I had not gone far before I came to the conclusion that one of the young men should be eliminated as an active party in the crimes. He had not participated in the other breaks, and had been drawn into this one less of his own volition than through his unrestrained admiration for a schoolmate. His own story, told to me under the stress of genuine grief, established his identity as a secondary figure in the plot very clearly.

Deprived of his father by death when a small child, and brought up on his grandfather's farm, he had begun to earn his own living at the age of fourteen, in order that he might assist his sister, who was fitting herself as a teacher in the State Normal School in Connecticut. A year later the grandfather died, and he was forced to seek a home elsewhere. He had been driving a milk wagon, but he obtained employment now with a lumber company, and received a wage of $7.50 a week. Of this sum he paid $3 a week for room, breakfast and supper, and upon many occasions he went without his dinner in order to send money to his mother and the sister. The lodging-house where he lived during this period was of the worst sort, and the common resorts of his fellow boarders were poolrooms, saloons, gambling-houses and places of even more evil resort; yet he kept himself clean, and remained there until his sister was self-supporting.

They talked the matter of his own education over many times, and he determined to better his condition. He left the lumber yard to learn the trade of a machinist, and he began to study with a correspondence school. This latter fact brought him to the attention of a teacher in a private school for boys, who became interested in his efforts, and advised him to enter the school, offering him work for his board and tuition. The youth accepted the offer gladly. He left the machine shop for the boarding-school; waited on table, looked after the laundry, and did repairing and odd jobs that kept him occupied from six in the morning until ten at night. The athletic committee drafted him to strengthen the baseball team, and he became its catcher and captain.

There was another player, Ned Kenwood, who had a rich grandfather and such personal possessions as an automobile registered in his own name, and a bungalow camp in the country. He became the friend of the captain of the team, and took him home with him, and had him for holiday trips to the camp. One does not need be told what this meant to a boy whose early years had been spent on a farm, and whose working age had begun at fourteen. It was the sudden realization of many things that had seemed forever beyond his reach.

One day, when the two young men were discussing the subject of adventures, and the scant opportunity for excitement in modern life, Kenwood made the statement that he had committed two burglaries, and that he had done it solely for the love of the sensation. He had not taken anything of great value, but he had faced the risk of detection, and had been entirely successful, the police believing it to be the work of a real burglar. He spoke of the matter so lightly that the sturdy young fellow who had gone without his dinners to send money to the women of his family was not shocked by the recital, but rather admired his audacity.

This conversation occurred in November, during the Thanksgiving holidays, and Kenwood did not refer to the matter again in the weeks that immediately followed. In January and February, however, working by himself, he began operations in another city, making the run in his car under cover of the night, and returning with knives, revolvers, cameras and photographic supplies, which he distributed as gifts among his friends at the school.

Late in May, desiring films and chemicals for developing them,—articles that he might have purchased anywhere, and within his allowance,—he invited his friend to accompany him and see the ease with which a place could be entered. He even boasted that he would rob a store already burglarized.

The captain of the ball team accepted the invitation. They placed a ladder against the rear of the building at midnight and entered by a window; and while they were within a passing patrolman discovered their means of entrance and sent in a call for assistance. Kenwood, masked and armed like a dime novel burglar, heard the ladder creak and discovered police ascending it. He led the way to the front door and unlocking it, sought to escape. Police with revolvers in their hands met them there. On the morrow their self-made sensation spilled over into the newspapers.

It was not difficult for me to determine that while the captain of the nine was technically an accessory to the crime, the real burglar was young Kenwood. Indeed, I was so certain of the soundness of the former, that I recommended probation for him as a matter of course, and after he had reported to me two or three times, and had obtained employment through his own efforts, I said to him: "You need not bother to come again unless you wish to do so of your own accord. I know that you will make good, and the next time we meet it will not be as officer and ward, but as friends. I will be glad to hear from you in that capacity as often as you want to call or write."

After the indictment he had been released under bonds furnished by Kenwood's grandfather, and another classmate had opened his home to him; for of course the arrest of the young men automatically closed the doors of the school against them. The wealthy merchant likewise offered him a position in one of his stores when probation was assured, and I rather admired the spirit in which the youth declined, preferring to seek a place for himself. He was no stranger to work, and he had no trouble in getting it. Before many months he wrote me that he had entered the employ of a physician who had specialized in X-ray work, and hoped to become his assistant. He is now a member of this man's home, and socially accepted by the latter's family. We may dismiss him from any further reference in this story. At the present time he is a student at Harvard University, and I fully expect that he will make his mark in life.

But young Kenwood, the heir to a chain of twenty-six stores, could not be taken on trust so easily. His environment had been of quite another sort, and the motive for his crimes had been established. It would never do to excuse him with the statement that he had turned burglar merely to have

a little fun in his leisure moments, because the world
has seen that type developed to its next stage, where
it becomes the profligate and spendthrift, and a
menace to society.

Inquiring into his antecedents to discover
whether he was inherently vicious, or merely reckless and irresponsible,—a duty not always agree-
able, but often necessary,—I learned that while the
grandfather was a man of strong character, and
highly developed in his business, the young man's
mother was of a weaker type, and only a passive
factor in the home. Her marriage had been the
result of a romance with a clerk employed by her
father, and the union had not been entirely satisfactory to her family. And their offspring had been
this son who, at nineteen, was backward in his
studies, derelict in his social duties, and who had
turned to strange paths in his search for excitement.

But both the father and the mother were deeply
concerned now, and the grandfather was ready to
move heaven and earth to save his heir; but since
they had been able to exert so little influence over
him before, I did not feel that I could safely recommend ordinary probation, and certainly I did not
want the world to point to this as another example
of the power of money. The question finally resolved itself to whether or not I could administer
some shock to this young man that would bump him

out of the lap of luxury, so to speak, and land him on the hard, stern realities of life; and both the Court and the grandfather agreed to accept any disposition of the case that promised to accomplish this end.

I do not know whether Rudyard Kipling, when he wrote "Captains Courageous," based the story upon fact or theory, but I have an opinion that he gathered his data of the Gloucester fishermen first hand, and that such a scion of a rich man as he portrayed would undergo just about the same experiences in real life as he gave to him in the pages of the narrative. In any event, I determined to try a similar cure upon Kenwood; and so I shipped him before the mast in the bark *Windrush*, on a seventy day trip to Buenos Ayres.

There needs be good stuff in any young fellow to stand a voyage in a sailing vessel in these days of steamships, and this trip, as it turned out, developed all the traditional obstacles of the sea. It was a beautiful day in July, the year 1913, when Kenwood went aboard the *Windrush*, but the first night out the bark ran into a deep fog, and ere long heard the distant bellow of a fog horn.

Only those who go down to the sea in ships can realize the menace of an approaching steamer in the fog. The man at the wheel of the *Windrush* brought her course about, only to come up into the face of the unseen, approaching steamship. The crew was piped to quarters, and again the hoarse bellow of the horn sounded, still nearer than before. Then out of the gray night loomed the bulk of the powerful liner, and Kenwood, the owner of an automobile, a bungalow and a rich grandfather, saw Death sweep by in its sea-shroud, and he realized something of what real life was. The *Windrush* escaped as by a miracle, and in the morning the fog cleared; but Kenwood had received his first shock, and it sobered him.

Fair winds carried the bark to the "Line," and then failed her, and she lay becalmed for three weeks. And Kenwood worked. He toiled at ordinary, ugly tasks of the sea until he mourned the day that the Court released him on probation. A clean, easy life in prison seemed preferable, even, to these incessant tasks under men who had lived the open life of the ocean highways, and held in contempt their weaker brethren of the effeminate cities.

Seventy days out brought the *Windrush* to a wharf of the second class in Buenos Ayres, and her crew were kept busy unloading the cargo of lumber. Then the sailors were given shore leave, and Kenwood started out with them to see one of the world's greatest cities. They got as far as the outer fringe of the dives that line the water front; which is as far as sailormen ever venture in a foreign port.

"I had read a lot about Buenos Ayres, but I changed my opinion as soon as I got ashore," Kenwood recorded later. "It is the worst place I was ever in for drink and what goes with it, and I was glad when we took a cargo of bone for the sugar refineries, and set sail for Philadelphia."

On the return voyage the work began to grow less irksome. His muscles had begun to harden, and the food no longer seemed coarse. "In fact, I rather like the life," he wrote in his diary. "We have caught a lot of fish, and things appear to be going well."

So they were, until Cape Hatteras was reached. Then, on the first day of January, a series of strong gales set in, and for almost four weeks the crew wore oilskins by night and day, for the mountains of waves swept over the deck again and again, and life became a desperate struggle to ride the storms.

The coal supply ran down to one ton, and they watched that disappear through the galley stove. The wood pile gave out, and it became necessary to tear out the lining of the after deck-house and use it for fuel. The food ran so low that Kenwood was grateful for his cup of tea, two thin slices of bread and a piece of fat salt pork three times a day. "I can see our finish in about nine days," he wrote grimly.

Yet here was real excitement, such as he had not dreamed of in the days when he had craved sensa-

tion, and had sought it by turning burglar.   Here
was Death in a new form, marking off the days of
life by so many cups of tea, so many thin slices of
bread, so many more pieces of fat, unpalatable pork.
The past year must have reeled through his memory
in review as he faced the brine-drenched, bitter reality of his new life.

Cape Hatteras has ever been a dreaded place for
the sailing ships.   It is the easternmost point of
North Carolina, a sandy insular spit, or narrow
beach, separated from the mainland by Pamlico
Sound.   No land south of the Capes of the Delaware stretches so far out into the Atlantic.   The
Gulf Stream, in its eastern and western vibrations,
often flows within twenty miles of the cape, crowd-
ing toward the shore the coasting vessels.   The
difference of temperature between the hot airs of
the Gulf and the breezes from off the land engender
frequent commotions in the atmosphere, and no
point on the coast is more noted for its dangerous
storms.   Nine of them, one following upon the
heels of another, beat and buffeted the stout *Windrush,* though she had been built against just such a
trial as this.   Her sails, made from the strongest
known weaves, began to be torn to shreds.   Three
of them were completely blown away.   At best she
could only hold her course, but without making any
headway.

There came a day when the captain called the

crew aft and told them that he had been twenty-five days in trying to make three hundred miles, and that the food supply was now so low that he felt compelled to turn about and seek the nearest port. With luck, he thought that Bermuda might be reached; and he trimmed the course of the ship accordingly.

And then the storm subsided, the wind changed, and the captain realized that he had given up a day too soon. He ordered the *Windrush* brought about, and made a new attempt to get around the Cape.

The men, exhausted by the long physical and mental strain, rebelled and threatened to mutiny. They said that to take another chance was to risk starvation, when the Bermuda course offered a safe retreat. The captain, facing the odds, promised the first man who dared disobey him irons for the balance of the voyage, and won the day by sheer nerve.

Kenwood, in the hour when, armed with mask and revolver, he had walked into the arms of the police, had experienced only stage heroics compared with the grim reign of law upon the high seas that followed until the bark, on the twenty-ninth of January, sighted a tug sixty miles off the Delaware River, and was towed to port.

"For the first time in a month I had a real night's sleep," the young man recorded in his diary.

On the following day he was paid off and left

the *Windrush,* with very kindly feelings for the men who had faced death with him. His father was awaiting him at the wharf, a hired automobile and chauffeur at his call, so that they might catch the first train home.

"I'm sorry, but I have business first at the British Consulate," said Kenwood when he was urged to hurry into the automobile.

"Business at the Consulate?" repeated the father, detecting a new note of responsibility in his son's words.

"Yes. I did a service for the consul in Buenos Ayres, and was told to collect two dollars here."

"I will reimburse you myself," the father replied as he hustled him into the machine. "This auto is costing me six dollars an hour, and I have had it for some time already."

But the point did not escape him that the son had learned the value of money; and when I sat down with him a few days later to talk over the experiences of the voyage, I realized how foolish it would be to send him back to school again. He had entered the world of men who toiled, and that was the only place for him hereafter. I advised him to go to work for his grandfather; and he became a shipping clerk at $1 a day.

He has made good since then, and gained his first promotion. I have concealed his identity in this narrative; and yet there is nothing in it for which he need blush, because youth and early manhood form a period that projects a Cape Hatteras into many a man's life. It is not what storms we encounter in those impetuous years, but rather how we weather them. The stout old *Windrush* in one brief voyage came near to a fatal collision, lost three of her sails, and all but starved her crew; yet she does not show a mark upon her to-day as she goes about her business, and not a word is said against her character as a ship.

So it is with the young man who seems to walk in the face of disaster for a time, but who ultimately finds his course and makes his home port without serious damage. What folly to send him to prison when he may still be saved! What a crime it would have been to dismantle the *Windrush* because she failed to make Cape Hatteras without a desperate struggle!

CHAPTER IV

THE SAVING POWER OF HARD WORK

I find myself, after concluding the previous chapter, recalling many cases in which a sea voyage has seemingly wrought a man's salvation, and it may be worth while to go further into this often effective, if always unofficial, form of corrective treatment. I am satisfied that the theory upon which it is based has proved sound.

The sea has ever held a lure for young men, and doubtless always will, and my appeal is to the imagination of the young fellows whom I hope to aid, holding out to them the promise of foreign ports, of strange ships upon the high seas, of adventures to be encountered there and not to be met upon the land. But in my own mind I have never once lost sight of the fact that the saving power of the sea is in the hard work that it gives to those who sail its ships. Toil that brings weariness at the end of the day, and deep sleep as its reward, is a remedy for the idle rich and the idle poor alike. As somebody has sagely remarked, the devil seldom finds work for busy hands.

Thomas Bullock, whom I found under indictment one day for breaking and entering a railroad station, seemed to offer the very opportunity of assistance for which my office was created.   He was twenty years old, a native of Massachusetts, the son of respectable parents, and had no court record. A colored youth whose acquaintance he had made, and who, as it appeared later, had committed larceny before, planned the burglary and had drawn him into it.   The sum of money that they obtained from the venture was only $22, and the Court offered to release them on probation if they would go to work and make an early restitution of the sum unlawfully taken.   Both of the defendants accepted these terms with gratitude, and the colored youth made good within a few weeks.

Bullock himself went out in search of work as soon as he was permitted to leave the court-room. As the insurance men would say, he looked to me like a good risk.   While his parents were easy-going in their home discipline, they were religious people, and the young man himself went regularly with them to a church noted for the piety of its members.   He would come to my office in the Court House, dressed in the clean overalls and jumper of a milkman's assistant, and tell me of the progress of his work, and of his desire to make a good man of himself; but he never brought a dollar of the money that was to make restitution for what he had stolen.

After a time I determined to make a personal investigation of his case,—for I had not then acquired an assistant to do home visitation work, and was depending upon office reports so long as the probationers appeared to be keeping faith with me,— and at the first opportunity I looked up Bullock at his own house.   I did not find him in.

"At work?" I inquired of his mother.

"No," she admitted.   "He has not been able to find anything since you took him on probation."

"Where did he work before?" I asked, concealing my true feelings.

"Why, he has never been able to find work that he likes since leaving school," she explained; but hastened to add that Thomas was a good son.   He was not unwilling to work, only there didn't seem to be the right place for him.

When I confronted Bullock with these facts, he confessed that he had arrayed himself in the overalls and jumper whenever he visited me in order that it might appear that he was working as I desired; and he seemed very sorry, and promised me that he would find a real and tangible job at once. But he failed to do so; and to see if the shock of a short imprisonment would not arouse him to his senses, I surrendered him for eight days, and he was duly locked within a cell.

He seemed to understand and appreciate my motive fully, and while in jail availed himself of the opportunity to read many of the good books that were to be found within its library. So far as I could discern, his brief term of incarceration passed quite agreeably, and he thoroughly enjoyed his unexpected course in literature. And I was delighted to note the spirit in which he started forth to obtain a long deferred employment. He reported to me from day to day. He was always in pursuit of a job, but never quite came up with it. Indeed, he was the traditional variable approaching its limit, with half the remaining distance always remaining to be traversed.

I determined at last to put Thomas aboard a New Bedford whaler; for while there is a prevailing opinion that these famous old ships now exist only in the traditions of New England, they still do make a voyage upon occasion, and I have more than once turned the knowledge to my own advantage. I prepared Bullock,—not for what was really coming to him, but for what he thought was coming,—by hints at the vastness of the ocean, the dangers of the sport of whaling, and the admiration that he would excite among his friends upon his return. Physicians have assured me that the patient receives the greatest benefit from medicine when he takes it in a receptive mood; and it is my profession to save rather than to chastise.

So we put Thomas Bullock aboard a whaler, out of New Bedford for seas unknown, his personal effects done up in a hand parcel, and his ideas as to his personal rights well defined, if as yet untested by the new standards to which I was introducing him. Just before he sailed, I urged him to note his impressions of the voyage, to the end that we might study them mutually upon his return.

Thomas came back at the end of six months, covered with boils, but with $25 in real money, which he promptly gave to his mother, with the request that she make restitution of the $11 due the railroad, and keep the remainder for board that might be owing her. Naturally, I was eager to hear his story, and it was a matter of gratification to discover that whatever stern thoughts he harbored concerning the masters of whaling ships, he had none against me for committing him to one.

"I wished that I was home when only two days out," he told me. "To speak the whole truth, I would rather serve five years in jail than be out there for two weeks again."

Five years in jail, I at once surmised, appealed to the imagination of Thomas Bullock as nothing more serious than an unlimited course in good reading, undisturbed rest at night, and regular portions of food. Yet his comment was superficial, for it was already apparent that the change had been of benefit to him.

"But what was wrong with the sea?" I inquired.

"The food was wicked, and the cooking was poor

and filthy," he replied. "We sometimes got food not fit to eat. You don't get food there like you get at home."

Item one: Thomas had learned that home had a value, though he had done nothing so far to deserve it.

"But there were other pleasant features?" I suggested.

Bullock gave me a reproachful look. "When the captain wanted anything done he didn't say 'Please do this' or 'Please do that.' He would speak only once, and if you wouldn't answer, or come when he called, you would either get punched in the jaw or kicked."

Item two: Thomas had sought to shirk work aboard the whaler as he had dodged it on shore, and the world at sea being very small, had been hunted down and cuffed about for it.

"But that was during the hustle of whale hunting," I said. "There must have been little to do at other times."

"When we had nothing else to do, the captain exercised us in hoisting sails four hours a day," said Bullock reproachfully. "Talk about a trip around the world! This is a lesson that I won't forget as long as I live."

I have the record of his statements verbatim, and they are not lacking in vehemence upon this point. Yet Thomas Bullock really obtained more from that voyage than he realized at the time. It was adventure worth while, and not to be found on every trip in these days of a declining whale industry.

Five days out of New Bedford a catch of five was recorded, and that meant work cut out for everybody. Bullock himself was in one of the small boats, and thus recorded his impressions: "We came up with a whale and threw a harpoon into it, and then there was fun. It got mad and pulled us over the ocean for miles; and talk about your rides! I don't think there is in the United States an electric car, a steam train or an automobile that can run as fast as these whales swim. It was 10 o'clock at night when the small boats got back. We got up one morning and chased a whale for miles. It took three bombs to kill it."

Bullock's body developed and hardened under this work. He learned to be alert against danger, and quick in action. Whenever he saw the harpoon sink into one of these mosters of the sea, and felt its frenzied jerk on the rope, he knew as it raced away that there was the ever-present risk of sudden death for himself and the crew of the little boat. Back from the chase, sore from the exertion and hungry for even the plain fare of the ship, the youth of religious training must have begun to think more seriously of life, and make plans for the days when he would return to land.

The last whale of the voyage was being taken

when the disaster so often averted overtook the group of men whose racing oars had come up with it. It was the second mate's boat, and he always made the harpoon throw himself. Bullock watched him, for he was a man of great strength and skill, and he understood just how to trim the craft when the barb landed, and the victim made the first mad rush to escape. But this time the whale did not seek to escape, but turned suddenly upon her assailants. The harpoon had imbedded itself in a great mother of the sea, about to calf, and in fury she lashed her mighty tail, and the boat, smashed like an egg-shell, was overturned, spilling its occupants into the churning waters. The mate, injured by the blow, went down to his death. Bullock and his mates struggled in the sea until another boat from the ship came to their rescue, and they were picked up, chilled and exhausted.

These were the real impressions that Thomas Bullock brought back with him, and they sobered him, so that he came to an understanding of the true place that man fills in the universal scheme of things. For man must work and undergo privation,—even face death at times,—for no better return than a day's small wage; and those who toil at sea meet greater perils than those who labor upon the land.

As for Thomas, he determined to work hereafter upon terra firma, and he did not even linger within sight of the sea. His probation complete, he hurried inland in search of employment, and when last I heard from him, he was tilling the land and serving as janitor of the village church. It is pleasant thus to remember him, so well occupied in life that even his church ministrations are not without their financial return.

It may occur to many of you who read these chapters of the sea to question whether its life of privation and hard knocks is to be recommended in many cases. As I have pointed out in the two that I have cited, which by no means comprise all that have come within my experience, it is the unusual case that requires the drastic treatment, and life before the mast or aboard the faster moving ship is no insurance against crime.

Occasionally the sea has cast at my feet, figuratively speaking, some young man who has gone down under its temptations, and I have been forced to acknowledge that other side of the sailor's life. The story of Arthur Nulton, that I am about to relate as a contrast to that of Thomas Bullock, offers such a study; though I desire to add that it is not, in my opinion, a typical case. I have sent several young men into the United States navy and army, and have had no occasion to repent so doing; and yet I sometimes wonder whether it was not the knowledge of such facts as Nulton relates that influenced the Secretary of the Navy to abolish alcoholic drinks from the warships, even at the risk of having his action so widely misunderstood.

In passing through the jail in East Cambridge one day I found a young man in a cell there awaiting the session of the Grand Jury. He appeared to be in mental distress, and when I began to question him he broke under the inquiry and told me that he was a thousand miles from home, had been arrested on a charge of forgery, and was without money to engage a lawyer to conduct his defense. He added that he was nineteen years of age, and had but recently left the service of the United States navy.

His manner as he talked to me suggested a good home somewhere in the background, and I asked him to consider myself as his counsel, and relate fully the circumstances that had brought him into the trouble.

"They caught me with a check for $20 made out in the name of a stable keeper for whom I worked," he explained. "I made it out myself, but I had never tried to pass it, and I never intended to. I simply used it for a four-flush. I was in with a bad crowd, and though I was earning $11, I was often broke, and I would flash this check in the barrooms to make it appear that I could raise money any time I wanted it. Word got back to the boss, it didn't look right, and he had me arrested."

"You should have had some money coming to you when you left the navy," I ventured.

"I had $30, enough to take me home from the navy yard in Charlestown, where I got my discharge, but I thought I would work here for a time before starting back," he replied. "I found a job taking care of horses, but I began to drink, and the money didn't last long. I have a mother and a younger brother at home, and two uncles who are lawyers, but I have not cared to write to them."

Three years in the navy did not seem to have done very much for this young man, and before offering him any definite promise of assistance, I wrote to the school authorities in his home town, and to the pastor of the church where he said that he had been a regular attendant. They gave him an excellent reputation in their reply, and the sheriff of his county vouched for his character and standing at the time of his enlistment. Reassured by these facts, I visited Nulton again and requested him to write me a full account of his experiences from the time that he left his home. From this statement, written in the solitude of his cell, I have drawn the facts that follow.

At sixteen he was the typical boy of the Middle West, patriotic in his inherited instincts, and eager to join the navy that he had invested with romantic interest because it seemed so remote from his own state. His mother was not inclined to permit him to go at first, but her friends argued that the service was educational, and the opportunity to see the world one that might not come to him in later life. He enlisted at Minneapolis, full of enthusiasm for the new life, and half hopeful that the three years might bring him active service. Twenty-eight other recruits were sworn in at the same time, and the party entrained for Norfolk, via Chicago, a seaman gunner in charge.

Now the expense of this trip was of course on the Government, and by the time Chicago was reached several of the young men had exhausted their loose change, and were thirstily sighing for refreshment. This is an age that may be led to the soda fountain or diverted to the saloon, according to its leadership, and the seaman gunner's thirst was for beer, and he knew how to obtain it. He suggested that if the members of his detail were willing to live on a dollar a day while in the city, instead of the $1.50 allowed him by the Department, there would be $14 available for liquor. The majority of them consented.

"That is where I got my start at drinking," wrote the boy from Iowa. "I was very sick for a couple of days, but I was told that I would get used to it if I stayed in the navy. I pretty soon found out that I must drink to be one of the boys, or I would be left out of everything that had any amusement in it. This was during my three months at the training station."

In October of that year he joined the U. S. S. *Buffalo,* which was under orders to convoy the First Torpedo Flotilla to the Philippines. The voyage was made by way of Porto Rico, the Canary Islands, Gibraltar, Algiers, Malta and on through the Suez Canal; a picturesque route, and one that has kindled the imagination of many a lad from an inland state. But Nulton, a boy out of a good home, had not yet found himself. He was disappointed to learn that beer or gin was sometimes offered as the prize when there was a boat race or a contest coaling ship. He felt himself going wrong, but was not strong enough to place himself on the side of those who were total abstainers.

"When we got shore leave after a month or six weeks we always had plenty of money, and the first thing we did was to drink and visit the sporting houses," he recorded. "The drinking crowd managed the sports ashore and you had to be one of the bunch to stand in with them. There were some on board the ship who pulled through this all right, but it spelled ruin for others, and I was among the unlucky ones. I saw the thing through to the finish, and it had me nailed when I left the service. But I hope with God's help to get back where I was once in my life."

I do not know that this man's story should be

taken as fairly representative of conditions during the period of his enlistment, but I am certain that his confession is sincere, and since the European war has shown that the efficiency of a nation at war depends in a measure upon the sobriety of its fighting forces, it may be that he had a right to expect it under the American flag, and that in his realization that the standard was lower than he had been taught to believe, he became an easy follower of the more turbulent members of the crew. In his three years of service he saw India, Ceylon, China, the islands of the Pacific—all that the navy had promised him when it offered enlistment; but he deteriorated steadily, until finally he was discharged for "physical disability." I do not know what that may have meant in his case; but he went almost directly to the saloon when he returned to civil life, and in this brief time was already in the toils of the police.

But we saved him. He was less a criminal than a young drunkard, and to brand him with a sentence would be to stamp out the last vestige of his self-respect. His place was in Iowa, among the people who had held him in esteem; and so he was released on probation, and we sent him back to his mother, one of his lawyer-uncles forwarding the necessary money. He took the pledge, kept his probation, and the charge of forgery was never pressed against him. At the present time he is employed by a mercantile corporation in Chicago, and nobody there suspects how near his career came to ruin. His native state did not hold him long, because when he came to himself, he found that his three years of travel had really made him ambitious, and he sought the larger opportunity.

The emphasis upon this narrative is not to be placed upon the fact that a gunner in charge of recruits debauched them, and came near wrecking this young man's life, but rather upon the system of probation that found him in his cell, friendless and discouraged, and sent him back a thousand miles to his home, there to readjust himself and begin anew. Viewing the matter from its economic side, he did not belong in Massachusetts, and to have sentenced him to a penal institution would have been to add one more item to our expense of maintaining criminals. Had we failed to reform him there, we might reasonably have expected him to join the ranks of our criminals, and so fasten himself upon us permanently. Because he was a stranger among us, a short-sighted policy based only on economy would have given him an opportunity to leave the state at once, upon the threat of arrest if he ever returned; a course that might not have helped him at all. There are states in which this elimination is practiced, and it appears to solve the problem for the time being; but it accomplishes nothing for the country at large. We chose to consider it as a problem of the young man, rather than of the State, to the end that he might be rendered a profitable, producing citizen once more.

Such a creed occasionally calls forth a protest from the citizen whose mental vision has not been broadened by the larger view of the question. He phrases it concretely in such words as these: "You have the proof that a man has committed a crime, but when he says that he is sorry, you release him, and he finds that the transaction has been entirely to his profit. You are depriving the law of its power by removing the fear of punishment. Other men are likely to learn that they, too, can commit crime with impunity, and then escape the inevitable wages of sin that the centuries have taught them to expect."

This argument sounds reasonable, but it is not one that will bear analysis. In the first instance, there is almost no form of crime that is permanently profitable, and even the professional criminal would give up his business in disgust if an expert auditor sat down with him for an hour to check up his accounts. The majority of people who constitute any community live within the law throughout their lives, not because they fear the results of transgression, but because the normal man or woman knows that happiness and peace of mind are not to be gained in any other way.

It is the abnormal conditions that make for crime.

Arrest during this apprentice period creates an interval of suspended activity in which the man often comes to a realization of what he has done, and wildly seeks some avenue of escape back to the life of honest living. If we insist upon administering the punishment that has been earned, he may come from it chastened and still penitent, acknowledging the justice of his sentence, and ready to win back the place that he has lost in the world.

But the records of all penal institutions show this to be true in so relatively few cases that an impartial judgment upon the matter must find that the prisoner who serves a sentence undergoes a moral or mental deterioration, and seldom fully recovers his former status. His pride has been crushed. Too often he feels that the mark of "jail bird" has been placed upon him. And upon this fact the whole system of intelligent probation is based.

CHAPTER V

THE SLUM AS A BREEDING-PLACE FOR CRIME

The slum as it is known in the great metropolitan centres does not exist in smaller cities; and yet its counterpart is there in smaller duplicate, and we can trace the same evils to it. For the poorest quarter of every city breeds crime, and to abolish it would be to reduce temptation to a minimum. Saloons prey upon the run-down tenements; the unemployed and those of irregular occupation are forced to take refuge there; manners are lax and morals often corrupt; upon every side are the influences that insidiously weaken the growing boy, offsetting the training that he is receiving in the public schools for five hours out of the twenty-four.

We need not concern ourself with the fact that in these slum tenements honest families do live, bringing up their children in the fear of God and the law, as they struggle against adverse economic conditions; or that from them sometimes come boys who in later life rise to distinction. These are exceptions. The poorest quarter of every city is a recruiting centre for the jail, the poorhouse and the asylum, and the duties of a probation officer call him there with such regularity that he soon comes to look upon it as one of the recognized haunts to which crime may be traced.

It was from such a place that Tom McGrath had come, and it was there that I went in his behalf when the opportunity came to give my opinion as to whether it were worth while to try to save him by probation. He was awaiting his trial for breaking, entering and larceny.

If ever a home,—or the lack of one,—marked a youth for a criminal, it seemed to have done so in this instance. Tom was only sixteen years old when the police finally decided that he was a hopeless offender, and must be sent through for sentence. Although little more than a child, and weighing only seventy-nine pounds, he was prematurely old, and a graduate of the streets, when the judge who heard his case in the Police Court sentenced him to the Lyman School. The lad did not want to go there, and shrewdly appealed his case, which brought him before the Superior Court at its next session.

But in the interval he found a friend, and it was a successful young business man, socially well known and a graduate of Harvard University, who appealed to me to have the boy placed on probation. He told me that he had a farm in New Hampshire to which he proposed to send him.

Tom McGrath's father was a drunkard and a loafer, who years before had taught his young wife to use liquor in their home. The woman had become intemperate at the time of the boy's birth, and within a year had been arrested, and was now on probation. Moreover, there was another son who had served a term in the Reformatory, and was now doing time in jail. Coming from such an environment it seemed folly to expect any good from this under-nourished boy, whose entire family were pushing him into crime, and I realized that the police would not concur in a request for probation.

The case came to trial, and the evidence went in. The police gave the boy a very bad record, and virtually said that he had gone the limit with them in the face of repeated warnings. They believed that for his own good he should be given a sentence. I looked about the court room, and I saw there the young Harvard man who had left his business for the day, and who earnestly wanted the release of this waif, because he believed that he could be saved.

At that time the experience of a private citizen voluntarily coöperating with my office was a new one, and I told the judge the circumstances, and made the suggestion that we give probation a trial in this instance, and note what came of it. He agreed somewhat reluctantly, and we took Tom from the room, openly grinning in the faces of the police.

A writer has observed, somewhat pitilessly, that virtue transplanted from the country to the city often grows into vice; but if this is so, one should add that a child rescued from the vice of a city slum and transplanted in the country may regain the virtue that should be his by right. We sent Tom Mc-Grath a full hundred miles from his home, and I waited for evil or good report concerning him.

He had been addicted to the use of cigarettes in the city, in spite of the public statutes forbidding it, but he gave them up of his own accord on the farm. He began to eat and sleep regularly, and at the end of two months he had gained fifteen pounds in weight. He was very proud of this fact. He seemed to accept it as the visible evidence of his reformation. Willingly he worked at the tasks of the farm, and wrote me the news of his shingling a barn as though he had done it unaided. He began to go to church, though a drive of seven miles was necessary to find a chapel of his faith. At the end of fifteen months he returned to us rugged and clean, a different lad from the one who had been sent away.

His probation was ended, and I had no further hold upon him, though I might have wished that he would remain in the country indefinitely. Very few of our criminals ever come from our farms; and this is true the country over. But his mother wished him with her again, and her claims upon him were not to be denied entirely. Perhaps, after all, he may be the means of her own regeneration; for a woman who has been branded with the curse of rum is weak above all others, and her salvation is not to be attained by any ordinary means. If he can reconstruct his home out of his experiences on the New Hampshire farm, then he will be doing a duty to his own people quite as much as did Kenwood when, brought up abruptly in his career, he returned to do a man's work.

But let us study the environment of the slum at closer range. There is a young man, only nineteen years of age, serving a sentence of a term of years for burglary in Massachusetts at the present time. So far as I know, he holds the record for the crime in which he has specialized, having no less than two hundred charged to his account. Possibly he is not guilty of all of them, but that number of breaks so closely resemble his handiwork, and are so well identified with burglaries to which he has confessed, that he has been given the benefit of the doubt in lieu of evidence to the contrary.

He is known as The Axeman, because his favorite method has been to smash his way into the shop or the house that he desired to rob, gaining an entrance through the basement; and he is still rather proud of the title, though he now expresses sorrow at the failure of his life, and protests that when he is released it will be to redeem his career. I have talked long and earnestly with The Axeman since he began to serve this sentence, and together we have gone into the question of what prompts the native born American boy to commit crime. He has written for me the narrative that follows, and I should add that it has not been done for the purpose of promoting some future petition for parole, but solely as his warning to other young men who may have read of his exploits, and looked upon him as a daring and successful criminal up to the day of his final arrest. He knows whereof he speaks. His are inside, elementary facts.

What surprised me at first in looking into his antecedents was to learn that he was the only son in a family of ten children, all New England born, and with the parents still living. It seemed unusual to find a boy, with so many sisters to shelter him, turning so early to crime, until I realized what the economic problem of that family might have been, with the father competent to command only a day wage.

"I do not remember my early life until I was eight years old," The Axeman wrote. "I was then living in the Brick Bottom in Somerville, Massachusetts, a very tough section."

The Brick Bottom, as it is known locally, would resent being called a slum, and yet it is a quarter where poor people seek their homes, accepting the dead level of its monotony as a fair reflection of the lives to which they are committed.

"And it was in the Brick Bottom that I learned to be bad," he confessed. "I recall many of the things that I was taught by the older boys. My first youthful crime was to steal tonic for them. They would put me through a window into the room where it was kept, because the opening was small, and I would bring it out to them. Later I was sent to roll barrels out of a shed, and the older boys would take them, and they would give me a penny when they had made a sale. It was the first money I ever had, and it made me feel rich to be earning it."

Here was a typical slum gang, seeking out petty loot and conniving how to obtain it with the least risk, and this boy was not the only criminal that went from it to the larger world. "Oh, no. I have kept track of those older boys. Every one of them has served time or is now in prison. They not only put themselves there, but they put lots of more young fellows there with them."

The gang breeds truancy as it develops minor crime. It is always to the slums that the truant officer goes in search of the boys whose public school attendance has become irregular, and upon one of these occasions he was looking for the boy who had begun to steal. Sensing the problem of the home, he advised the parents to have the lad sent to the Middlesex County Training School, an admirable institution for constructive work. They gave their consent. It meant one less mouth to feed and one less child to clothe.

And the boy, on his part, discovered a new type of school. There were more than two hundred boys there, who were divided among several brick buildings, each one as attractive as a model public school. There were broad acres where the lads raised the vegetables that they ate. There was a pine grove and a ball field. There was a band to which any boy musically inclined could aspire, and it was invited to give concerts all over the county. There were a few rules, and one lost his marks for violating them, but there was no such thing as corporal punishment, and for a long time there had been no fence about the grounds.

This boy from Somerville led a healthy life while at the school; became a trombone player in the band; made progress in the schoolroom; and finally gained his release to find his parents in a little better circumstances, and living in another city. His mother was delighted at the change in him, and urged him to continue his studies. He did so, and was graduated at the age of sixteen. Then the family fortunes waned, and the father decided to return to Somerville.

"From the day I left the county school until we moved back to Brick Bottom I never missed a day at school or stole one thing," the boy wrote. "But back in Somerville I fell in with the gang again, and began to go wrong."

The family made another change of residence to

Cambridge, and the son found employment in a piano factory at $8 a week. He wanted to keep straight, and he gave his earnings to his mother for a time. "But I soon got in with a crowd in Brookline Street," he continued. "One of its members was the son of a police inspector, and we thought we had things our own way; but he is doing time now in the Concord Reformatory. These fellows were not working, but they managed to get enough money to take care of themselves. I left the factory and hung around the streets with them, throwing the dice, and stealing from time to time. Then the police began to pick us up one by one. They sent me away to the Shirley Industrial School."

This is another excellent state institution in which an intelligent effort is being made to rescue flotsam from the slums. It is run on the cottage plan and the merit system, and the idea that a boy has been sent there for punishment is entirely subordinated to the effort that is made to aid him. This youth found himself once more in a wholesome, honest atmosphere. He took up music again and soon found his place in the band. He played on the football team and became captain of the baseball nine. Nor was the personal element in his life lacking. His room was in Cottage No. 2, where the boys were under the direction of Mr. and Mrs. William Waller. "I never knew a better man or woman," was his tribute to them. "We called her mother,

and Mr. Waller father because they were so kind to
the boys. Mr. Waller would often take me aside
and say, 'Jim, when you go home, if you ever need
a friend come to me. I know that you have been a
good boy under my care.'"

He left the school with the highest recommendation, and having learned the trade of cook while
there, found work in a city where he was not known.
Had he remained there, all might have gone well,
but he quit work after a time and returned home.
There he met some of the members of the old gang,
who had done time and been released. They were
not reformed. They were merely shrewder in planning their crimes now, and confident that they could
escape being caught. They counted him as one of
their number, and began to invite him to join their
ventures.

But even then he recalled the words of Mr. Waller and made a trip to Shirley for advice. His old
friend told him what he must do to keep straight.
He returned home, intending to do so. But the
gang had pulled off another job and nobody had
been caught. They told him just how it was done;
and he turned burglar and was not arrested. In
due time he became the recognized leader, and then
began to branch out for himself.

He shifted the scene of his operations from one
city to another, until half a hundred trained police
were trying to find the mysterious burglar who

worked with such impunity. He fooled not only them, but a young girl with whom he fell in love at this time. His own pals began to fear him, and one of them who crossed his trail at the wrong angle carried away a bullet from his pistol in remembrance of it. The police were now very close upon his trail, though he did not suspect it, for they had found a thumb print upon a window after one of the robberies, and they had such a thumb recorded against just such a day, and knew the man to whom it belonged.

My information concerning his exploits at this period are not drawn from his own confession, but from police sources. He is significantly reticent concerning them; though whether from reasons of personal interest or because he no longer takes pride in them, it is not pertinent to observe. But his comment upon his career is quite worth repeating:

"No matter how brilliant or wise or shrewd you think you are at this game, you always leave your tracks behind you. I do not say this from my own experience alone, but I have talked in prison with one of the world's greatest crooks."

There is a certain flamboyant pride in this last statement, and yet it is offset by the conversation that did take place between them:

"He looked at me for a moment and said in a normal tone: 'First time in, eh? What do you expect to bring with you?'

"I told him a three spot.

" 'Bank work?' he asked.

" 'No, just a little foolish work I did, and they got sore and pinched me,' I explained.

" 'Sure, they always do,' he said.

" 'Do what?' I asked.

" 'Pinch you. You are nothing but a kid, but you ought to have known better, for you have an education. They always get you in time.'

"I smiled at this, and I said, 'Well, you have been foolish yourself, and what do you expect to get for a sentence?'

"He said he didn't know, and he told me about his life. He had lived a very bad life, and he had been a counterfeiter, yet once he had given up the crooked game for five years, to marry a woman whom he loved. But he said he couldn't make it pay, and he went back, and they caught him and sent him up for fifteen years. But he was so clever at his business that I couldn't see how he ever came to be pinched, and I told him so.

" 'You pinch yourself the minute you begin this crooked game,' he told me. 'The game itself does it. It pinches you because it is strong. It does not fit in with this world. Take my word for it, anybody who plays the crooked game is a sucker, because it can't be made to pay.' "

"Can it?" I asked The Axeman when I had read his confession.

"It can't!" he replied without hesitation. "Among the gang and the police I have the reputation of having made a lot of money as a crook, but it never did pay. It can't be done."

"But if it never did pay, why did you so often return to the life?"

The question appeared to bring a bad taste to his mouth, for he turned it over bitterly, until it brought him finally back to the slum.

"There is an underworld in every large city, and the harm is done there," he said. "In Boston it is in the South End. Around Dover Street, in the low-class pool rooms and the Jewish card dens from three to five hundred crooks are made yearly. A boy makes a big mistake to go to such places."

Even as he spoke he forgot that he was the successful crook of two hundred burglaries, whose deeds were still related in this underworld of thieves who aspired to achieve what he had done, and he burst forth with mingled hope and complaint:

"I am only a young boy, after all, and the world is before me. I have everything to live for; a sweetheart, a mother, a father and sisters. I ought to have known it wouldn't pay. It is too late to say this when you are behind prison bars. If those big boys had not taught me to steal when I was so young, I would not be here today. It is a great deal easier to get into trouble than it is to get out; and all the men who are in here say the same thing."

Our penal institutions are filled with these men who feel remorse when they are shut apart from the world; but in many cases nothing comes of it. The first revulsion of feeling over, the majority of them sink to a dead level again. They have ceased to regard prison as a place of punishment or their term there as a degrading experience. The world whose laws they have violated having cast them off, they find here home of a sort and the society of their own fellows. They are sure of sufficient food, clean sleeping quarters, an allowance of tobacco, entertaining books to read and electricity for light. If their education is deficient, instructors are provided for them. Even the sentence to hard labor, so often cited by the newspapers, is a misnomer. There is no such thing as hard labor for them; in fact, there is not labor enough at certain times.

Notwithstanding these facts, there is a chance that The Axeman may redeem himself. His career has shown courage and spirit of a sort, and the odds that are to be placed against his salvation may appeal to him as a feat worth performing. Suppose that he does come out, and facing the world fearlessly, offer it this challenge: "I have been a notorious young burglar, guilty of many crimes. My former associates stand ready to take me back into their fellowship, and the police have little faith in my good intentions. Yet I am going to make good. I want the world to know who I am and to watch me while I gain a place in the esteem of honest men. Criminal statistics are against me. I intend to prove that they are incorrect. I will be as good a citizen as I was once an efficient burglar."

The psychology of life is such that many people would stand by this young man on such a platform. They would accept him because he made no effort to conceal his past, and they could throw about him the very influences that he will require to face the obstacles in his way.

In any event, we are not done with him when he has finished his sentence and obtained his release. He remains a problem for which we are responsible until we become certain that he will no longer prey upon society, but has indeed become one of its productive citizens again.

CHAPTER VI

SAVING THE BOY FROM A CRIMINAL RECORD

Since the passage of the Juvenile Delinquent Law in several States of the Union, the boy who violates the public statutes is no longer treated as a young criminal whose deed has set him apart forever from other youths, but he is given the benefit of every error in his environment and early training. Wise legislators have discerned among the young who have gone astray the real salvage that is to be sought by the probation officers, and have provided for the trial of persons under seventeen years of age at a special session of the Court, where they are not in contact with adult offenders, are shielded from publicity, and where, after a thorough inquiry into the circumstances of their misdemeanor, they are released under conditions that do not enter their name upon the police records.

It may be said in passing that this law is not considered to be entirely successful in its operation in the large cities. They who criticise it are the police officials, who find themselves sometimes hampered in seeking to put a stop to the numerous petty infractions of the law. The small boy has come to believe himself immune in the States where the most humane legislation has been enacted in his behalf, and calling to account in a friendly court oftentimes has no more lasting effect than a similar interview in the office of a schoolmaster who has abolished corporal punishment.

There is some reasonable ground for this criticism, but we must not lose sight of the larger side of the question. Locking up boys in cells over night and bringing them before the full machinery of the courts for sentence did not check their infractions of the law under the old system, and we must look for results from another angle. How many of these bad boys really go straight after they are placed on probation?

I have made a detailed study of the cases of one hundred boys who were placed under my care as a probation officer within a given period, and as an interval of several years has elapsed, it is possible to speak with some authority concerning their subsequent history. Their ages when I took them were as follows: One was nine years old; three were ten; five were eleven; five were twelve; fifteen were thirteen; fifteen were fourteen; nineteen were fifteen; thirty-seven were sixteen. In these successive years one may discern the increasing temptations of boyhood, and the diminishing influence of the home.

In the list of offenses, assault with a dangerous

weapon, attempt to commit larceny, larceny from a building, robbery, unlawfully taking a team, stubborn child and unnatural acts claimed one each. Tresspass, larceny from person and immorality accounted each for two more. There were three cases of assault and battery and a like number of ringing in false fire alarms. Four boys had been arrested for larceny and five for disturbing the peace. Then came breaking and entering and larceny with eighteen offenders, simple breaking and entering with twenty-seven more, and larceny with a like number. To sum up, the attempt to steal had brought seventy-seven boys before the court.

These boys were all taken on probation, and upon terms to meet their special needs. In one case we appealed to the jury for some farmer willing to take a boy home with him, a request that met with a prompt response. A truant was found to be suffering from defective eyesight, and when I further made him an assistant truant officer for the school, he became a model pupil, holding his fictitious office with great credit. Another boy was sent to a sheep farm, far from city influences, while a fourth was required to go to work and pay back $100 for damage that he had done. And so one might go on with these details.

The record of these hundred boys to-day is seventy saved, three with a fair record, nineteen since arrested, and eight surrendered for breaking their original probation. Was not the effort worth while?

I believe that the enforcement of our juvenile laws sometimes fails because of an error in judgment on the part of the probation officer. It does not follow that because the young offender is saved from a direct sentence, he is excused from all responsibility for the damage that has been done to property. If we can compel him to make restitution in some form, we are neither punishing him by the curtailment of his liberties, nor are we permitting him to enjoy full immunity. Let a case from my own experience point the moral to this.

Six young men in a country town, intent upon celebrating the night before the Fourth of July, set fire to an old barn, which contained agricultural machinery. Their bonfire thus ignited cost a property loss of a thousand dollars to the owner, and he caused their arrest, and desired that they be prosecuted as an example in the community. Arson is a serious crime, and punishment for it follows a man throughout his life. When sentiment within the town found expression, the public realized that the traditional license of the holiday had really been responsible for this unfortunate occurrence, and an earnest effort was made to permit a settlement and have the cases placed on probation. I agreed to this upon one condition; that the young men themselves make restitution to the owner of the barn, in proportion to their part in its destruction.

Five of the youths earned their money and made the payment within a year; the sixth, an orphan, was eight years in clearing his obligation, but he finally paid it in full. To-day one of the young men is a trusted clerk in a city bank, a second is the postmaster of a town, two are running a cattle ranch in Montana, another is a railroad brakeman, and the sixth is a chauffeur. Everybody has forgotten the fact of their arrest for an escapade; but would it have been passed over so lightly had we sent them to the Reformatory, where logically they might have gone?

I would not argue here or elsewhere that all boys who develop wayward tendencies can be saved by probation. If a certain number of men arrested in any state are found to be confirmed criminals, whom no law appears to restrain, and no institution reform, it needs must follow that such men were once boys, and that their vicious tendencies were inherited, or their habits hopelessly formed by early environment. There are authoritative writers who will dispute the statement that one inherits criminal tendencies, but none of them, I assume, will deny the fact that the children of defective parents are themselves often sub-normal.

But this is not always apparent in the early way-

wardness of the child. We accept him first as a
moral delinquent, temporarily led astray, but capable of being restored to normal living, and we feel
certain that intelligent treatment will save him.
The experiment fails, however, and the police bring
him back to answer to more serious offenses. We
now give his case more earnest consideration, turning him over to specialists in some state school organized to meet just such needs as his own. This
treatment has availed in other cases, but it fails
here; and again he is before the Court. But we go
on with our efforts to reform him, making use of
every agency that the state affords, oftentimes at
an increasing expense to the taxpayer; only to learn
in the end that we were dealing with a born criminal from the beginning.

Possibly we have such a case in Joseph Dulan,
whose career is not yet ended as I write. The telling of his story will answer the query that may have
arisen already in the mind of some reader, as to
whether it is not my purpose in these pages to bolster
up the argument for probation, ignoring the fact
that it is not effective in every case. I have no such
intention. The problem itself is far less simple
than that.

Dulan at nine years of age had found school so
irksome that a truant officer was detailed to look
him up, and he was entered as a pupil at the County
Training School. He was there for two years, well

fed, well clothed, properly exercised and instructed by interested teachers. I have seen so many boys lifted over the trying period in their lives and made into good citizens by this school that I know Dulan had his chance there, and should have given no further trouble.

Four and a half months of free life back in the city, and he was again in the hands of the truant officer, and had been recommitted to the county school. The father interceded for him after a time and obtained his release; but it was in vain, for he would not respond to parental authority, and when he was sent back for the third time, he remained for two years.

His age was now fourteen, and four important years of his life had been spent under special supervision in an effort to train him for good citizenship. He seemed to have come to his senses, and there was every reason to believe that he would find a place for himself in the world. As a matter of record, he had not been home more than six weeks when he was arrested on the charge of being a stubborn child; which meant that he was going with bad companions, would not work, and was hanging about the streets late at night. The Lyman School for Boys, a step on the way to the Massachusetts Reformatory, next received him.

"I was there a little over a year, and then they transferred me to the Reformatory," Dulan told me, relating his experiences six years later. He was then twenty years old, awaiting trial for stealing the horse of his employer. His parents were now dead, and his only living relative had given him up as incorrigible. Without friends or money with which to engage a lawyer for his defense, he had decided to plead guilty and take whatever was coming to him. I saw no reason why he should do otherwise, but as a matter of form I asked him to tell me of his life during the intervening years.

"Oh, I was at the Reformatory for about a year, and I worked in the Weave Shop," he said. "I had nothing against the shop or the men over me, but I couldn't seem to do the work as they wanted it. I kept getting locked up and losing my merits, and I got discouraged. I went to the superintendent and told him of my troubles, and he promised to take me out and give me another job; but things went on the same as before."

"How the same as before?" I inquired.

"Why, the superintendent did not change me. I went to him again about it. Then I decided to get out myself."

Dulan had become familiar with his rights as a young criminal, one may note, and considered himself being imposed upon. The habitual criminal comes to look upon these institutions as his own world, and he knows far more about them than does the law-abiding citizen who supports them.

"So you decided to get out. How did you accomplish it?"

"I started a small fire; just a handful of waste. No particular damage was done."

Of course not! Fortunately the blaze was discovered in the nick of time, or the lives of a hundred men might have been put in peril.

"They let you go out then?"

"They sure did. I was taken out for trial and sent to the House of Correction. They gave me three years, but I had won my point on them, because it was better to do that stunt than remain at the Reformatory for five years. I did my time there and then went out, and I hit the trail for New York to get a job."

Here, again, was Dulan's opportunity to turn his life to some account. Eight years of it had now been spent in county or state institutions, at a considerable cost to the community. New York, the great clearing house for men who must start life anew, had nothing against him, and asked only that he work. And opportunity was not lacking, for he was employed by turn as electrician, waiter, baggage porter and messenger about the wharves. He did not remain at anything very long, and presumably he did not perform his work any too well. After a time he returned to Massachusetts and was engaged as a teamster at $2 a day.

"I worked for a good man, and I don't know what

put it into my head to do him," he told me. "I worked honest for about three weeks, and then I had a few drinks, and I stole the team. The law doesn't take into account my not being sober, but there was no other reason for my doing it, and so I'm going before a jury and judge, all for a bit of foolishness."

I took Dulan's case home with me, so to speak. Did I owe him anything, since the state had devoted so many years to his reform, and had failed so completely? And yet as I pondered the matter, the fact occurred to me that this was his first real crime, the stealing of a horse, and he had committed it to no purpose, but because his brain had been muddled with liquor. Since institutional life could have no great influence upon him now, and he admitted his act and did not consider that it was fully criminal, it might be that probation would appeal to him as an opportunity to prove that his recent slip was only an error of judgment, and that he could maintain himself in the world.

When the case was heard in court I related his story to the judge, and proposed that inasmuch as he had never yet been placed on probation, he be turned over to my office to see what could be done for him. The judge assented to this, and I took Dulan from the court room, apparently grateful for the efforts that had been made in his behalf.

I was now thoroughly interested in the experiment, and I took him back to my own city that night, and made myself responsible for his lodging in a respectable boarding house, and on the following morning secured employment for him at a fair wage. If there was any gratitude in him, he owed it to me to make good.

But it was not in him! At the end of six days he drew what money was due him, got ingloriously drunk, and disappeared without paying his board bill. He had flung me over as lightly as he had the other agencies of the state that had sought to aid him. I settled his account, and then I set out to find him. Probation, though a gift, must be respected. It is not a charity to be cast aside like an old garment. Dulan had seen me at my best, and had misjudged me; now he had me angry.

When the police net of the state failed to find him I concluded that he had gone beyond our borders, but I counted upon his returning as he had done once before, and so I set a trap for him at the State House in Boston. There is a room there not often seen by the casual visitor to the historic building, given over to the Bureau of Criminal Identification. It is such a place as Mr. Sherlock Holmes might have visited with real pleasure; and curiously enough it seems better staged for a detective story than for the hunt of everyday criminals. A magazine editor told me only recently that the finger print situation was being overdone in the mystery plot;

but in real life it becomes a greater factor with each succeeding year in the pursuit of the burglar and the murderer.

To this office, then, I went, in my search for Dulan. It was a room lined on two sides with cabinet drawers, familiar since the card index system came into such universal use. The official in charge of the Bureau sat at a desk, with bundles of new finger prints all about him. His assistant, a young woman, sat at one end of a long table, a pile of finger print records in front of her. The only decoration upon the walls was a magnified print of somebody's thumb; a strange exaggeration of the lines to be found in the human digit. In the cabinets were the finger prints of twenty-five thousand criminals!

I was not so old in the work but that the latent, potent romance of this silent room appealed to me, and I stood for a moment unnoticed as I contemplated it. Its two workers were engrossed in their tasks. The man was recording a fresh print, his magnifying glass bringing out its arches, whirls, loops and radials, the primary classifications employed in arriving at the formula of the human hand. The young woman at the table was running her eye over the pile of selected cards, and quite likely her mind was dealing in such phrases as central and lateral pockets, or twin loops. Strange detectives, these modern hunters of criminals!

Another visitor entered; not lightly, as I had
done, but with a quick stride that took him to the
desk. He carried a flat parcel, which he opened
with deliberation and care, disclosing a window
pane, cut out from its frame. It was a dirty
pane, but upon it had been pressed the imprint of a
thumb as it was opened from the outside.

"See whether you know this thumb," said the man
briskly. "It's the only clue we have."

When the police register a man for future identification they press the fingers of his two hands,
spread apart, on a card, a special ink leaving the
record there. Then the four fingers of each hand,
drawn together, are registered, and finally his right
thumb is recorded alone. This thumb will sometimes track a man. It did in this case.

"Here we are," said the Bureau official after a
study of the glass and a search in his cabinets.
"Your man was arrested in New York for burglary,
and once in this state for highway robbery. Here
is his photo."

The officer grunted. "I passed him on the street
myself, within a week," he said. "The next time
he comes out of his hole we will have him."

It was time to state my own business. I asked
whether there was a record of Thomas Dulan's
fingers, and found it on file. The young man had
been registered at one of the institutions where he
had served time.

"If a duplicate set comes in from any source at any time, notify me at once," I said; and went my way. The months passed by; and it began to look as though Dulan had eluded me.

But one day a man who gave the name of Frank Whiteley was arrested for drunkenness and larceny, and sentenced to Deer Island for thirty days. He was finger printed there, and his card sent in to the Bureau of Criminal Identification, but when it was filed away, it was found to correspond with the card of Thomas Dulan. Beside it was my request of several months ago, and a notification was sent to my office. In a million hands there are no two persons that have the identical markings.

Whiteley served his time, but as he was about to leave the Island, an officer met him with a surrender warrant to take and deliver him to the sheriff of my county. We met on the day following.

"So you thought that you had fooled me, Dulan," I said.

"I had you fooled for a time," he said; and told me how carefully he had planned to keep beyond the arm of the law. He had taken refuge at first in the backwoods of Maine, where he had worked in the logging camps for eight months. There was not one chance in a thousand of catching him there. He had crossed the frontier into New Brunswick, and found employment there for another four months. He had spent a quarter of the next year in Maine again, and for six weeks had lived unmolested in New Hampshire. Then he had considered himself safe from further pursuit, had changed his name, and returned to Boston. For two weeks he had even worked within sight of the State House, where the trap had been so long set for him.

"But we got you," I said. "Breaking probation is one of the things that a man is not permitted to do in this state."

"I got drunk and they landed me," he answered. "I pleaded guilty so as not to attract any attention."

There was not another word to be said in his behalf, and I surrendered him and he was given six months in the House of Correction. He has learned that probation may be elastic, but that it is not snapped with impunity. But beyond that fact I do not feel certain that he has added any item to his knowledge of life. Only time and the finger-print records will show whether he has become an habitual criminal, or whether he has come to an understanding of the truth that the way of the transgressor is not worth while.

CHAPTER VII

THE SPIRIT OF WANDERLUST THAT LEADS TO CRIME

I stood in a Reformatory workshop one day where fifty young men, all of them barely past the voting age in the United States, were at work. They had been committed for various offenses, the most common of which was breaking and entering, and they represented nine nationalities.

"Wanderlust?" I said to the officer at my side. We had been speaking of the boys who came over in the immigrant ships without their parents.

"In many cases there is the spirit of adventure behind them," he admitted. "The married men who seek a home here have a definite purpose in coming to America. But with many of the others it is the wanderlust, I suppose, that prompts them."

"And they fall before the temptations of our large cities. They were not young criminals when they came over?"

"Let us give them the benefit of the doubt," he said. "The majority of them are just boys who have gone astray because they are away from the home influences."

Since that day many of these cases have passed

through my office, and I have been forced to set down the spirit of wanderlust as one of the causes that may develop crime. And it is reasonable to discuss this problem, since one so often hears the phrase: "We ought to have stricter immigration laws. Foreign countries are dumping their criminals upon our shores. The police records show it."

At first sight they do seem to indicate it, but a closer analysis divides the foreign born criminals into two classes; and they are identical with those of the native born. There are the professional crooks, who have found it advisable to leave their own land, and the occasional criminals, whose offenses often come under the head of accidental crime.

The wanderlust itself is not confined to young men who come to us from across the seas, though I have chosen such a case for this narrative. We find it among our own boys, for the school truant not infrequently becomes a tramp, whom necessity will some day make into a criminal.

When first I made the acquaintance of Charles Tower, whose story I am to relate, he was nineteen years old, and had lived already under two aliases. He was now awaiting trial on a charge of breaking and entering, and the official visitor of the State Board of Charity who wrote to me in his behalf added the footnote: "I fear that little that is good can be said of him, although those who do not know about him are apt to be favorably impressed when first seeing him."

I learned that he was seeking to have the charge against him placed on file, so that he might return to his home in England; but one can not obtain the consent of the Court to such a suggestion unless there is a special reason for such action, otherwise this country might be open to the charge of deporting criminals. It became my duty to look into the case very carefully.

On the very day that I undertook this task, Charles Tower received a letter from his mother in England. How many wandering boys have mothers, after all! And how often she comes to their aid in an hour of crisis in their lives, even though the seas roll between.

"Oh, Charles, what did you ever see in your life at home to make you go wrong?" this mother pleaded. "I was so delighted when I saw that the letter was from you to Frank that I opened it to get news of you; and God knows how I feel now, for I can't let Frank see it, and must bear my trouble alone. I must keep the shame to myself, though it breaks my heart. I have written to a lawyer in America to see the least that will get you out of trouble; and I will get the money somehow, even if I sell my clothes. I pray God to help you, for I cannot write more. Your loving but broken hearted mother."

I looked at this young burglar in a new light. "So you wrote home," I said.

"I wrote to my brother."

"You had a good home, I take it."

"We lived in a house called the Laurel Villa.   I have a mother and two brothers, and I went to a boarding school at one time, and was expected to enter an office later.   But I wanted to make my own living in my own way, and so I ran away when fifteen years old."

It required no further data to conclude that his adventure had not been entirely profitable.   Though prepossessing in appearance, and a ready talker, the life had begun to leave its marks upon him, and but for the letter from his mother I would have dismissed his case as one not likely to come within the scope of probation.   As it was, I drew his story from him, only to find it typical of those who live just beyond the pale of social responsibility.

When he had decided to run away from home, he had gone directly to a seaport and obtained a berth as assistant steward in a steamship.   For more than two years he sailed about the world, his thirst for new sights unappeased, his home apparently forgotten.   At length a ship in which he had taken service put in at Athens, and he obtained shore leave.   He formed an acquaintance with a Greek interpreter there, who advised him to remain ashore; so he deserted his ship and entered the

Greek's employ, who found him useful in acting as a guide to English and Americans. Under this competent instructor he became versed in the Athenian ruins; took parties of tourists inland; received liberal tips for his services, and during his free nights loafed among the cafés of the capital.

"And you never wrote home?" I asked him.

"I never wrote home," he answered. "The Greek had advised me not to, and I began to forget my own people."

The tourists whom he served as guide were often attracted by his youth and versatility. He had picked up a certain patter of the world, and had a ready story for those who were inquisitive as to his antecedents. One day an American who had taken an interest in him urged him to go to the United States. "You should not be satisfied with the life here or with these people," he said. "If you have your own way to make in the world, America is the place for you."

The romance of this suggestion appealed to young Tower. After all, he was finding life a very attractive adventure because he had the courage to leave the beaten paths and follow his own inclination. He shrewdly appraised the American—oddly enough he was from Missouri,—and undertook to work upon his sympathy. The upshot of it was that the tourist bought him a passage on an Austrian ship bound for New York. Even then he did not spend the voyage in idleness, for the captain's steward falling overboard one day and losing his life, Tower worked himself into the place thus vacated, and landed with fifteen dollars more than when he set sail.

In New York he lived comfortably until his money was spent, when he found employment at Trinity Mission House, where he remained for a year. Following this he did odd jobs for several months, and then went to Boston, where he decided to return to England in a cattle ship.   He signed as a member of the crew, but having several days' freedom before his services were required, he set out to spend the forty dollars that represented his savings.

"It was almost time to sail, and I had spent all but nine dollars, when late one night a police officer held me up and asked me where I was going," he told me.   "He didn't like the answers that I gave him, and took me to headquarters on suspicion.   I was locked up until morning, when I told my story again, and was just being released when two inspectors came in and looked me over.   They took me before a judge and had me sent to the State Farm.   I don't know to this day why they did it."

"They took you for a vagrant," I suggested. "You were not working, and had been hanging about the streets late at night."

"But I wasn't a vagrant," he protested.   "I had money in my pocket and a ship to go to."

This explanation did not sound plausible. Police at a seaport are too familiar with the adventures of sailor men not to investigate a story likely to excuse them, and a further inquiry drew the admission that two other young men had also been arrested in his company, and sent to the State Farm for the general good of the community.

"But they got their mothers to plead for them, and they were pardoned out in a few days," he continued. "I wrote Dr. Lewis and told him my whole history, and asked why I had been sent away for doing nothing. But he could do nothing for me."

Now Dr. J. F. Lewis was superintendent of the Division of State Adult Poor, and if Tower knew enough to write to him, and was turned down upon investigation, there was certain to have been less injustice in his arrest than he would have me believe. I recalled the letter from the State Board of Charity, to the effect that little good could be said for this young man. Somewhere along the line of his narrative he had begun to romance for me, and unless I kept my wits sharpened he would speedily turn my office to his own advantage.

"And Dr. Lewis would do nothing for you?" I said sympathetically.

"No. But dear Mr. Blackstone finally sent me to the Reformatory to learn a trade and reform. I was there for four months."

"To reform?"

He realized that I had caught him in a slip of the tongue. "I had a very good record there," he hastened to add. "All the officers were very kind to me, and I was finally permitted to go before the chairman of the Prison Commission and tell my story."

"Ah, that let you out! You had been arrested for no real crime, and the chairman ordered your release."

He eyed me thoughtfully for a moment, but my own manner was bland and innocent. "The chairman took the matter under consideration for a few weeks and then called to see me," he explained.

"What happened then?"

"The best thing he could do for me was to send me back to the State Farm, which he kindly did."

"But if you were being unjustly held, why did you not write home for help?"

"I finished my nine months in December with a good record, and reported to the State Board of Charity. I fully intended to go right home. I was given clothes and five dollars in money and told to keep away from all bad boys. I went over to the shipping office in Boston, but all the boats were filled up, and I returned and so reported to the Board. Mr. Flint in the office there told me he would get me on a boat through the influence of one of his friends, and told me what day to come back."

"That was your chance," I pointed out. "You

wanted to get out of the country, and here was a man who stood ready to aid you. Why, then, are you here to-day?"

He hesitated for a moment, and then said: "I met a pal on that day. We talked of making a break in Cambridge and went over at five in the morning. We broke a window in the place and went in, helping ourselves to pipes and things. Then we went over to Salem Street in Boston to sell them, and there a police inspector found us and arrested us. I told the whole truth to the police, and they promised to help me get out. I swear to God above that I will never do such a thing again, and if they will let me, I will go home. This has been a great lesson to me, and I will turn over a new leaf."

But his story had failed to convince me. Even after he had put it in writing, and added more fervent promises of reform, I could not rid myself of the feeling that he was seeking to escape a punishment that he deserved, and was merely play-acting to serve his own purposes.

Fragmentary as was the recital of his life since leaving home, there was nothing in it to indicate that he had ever performed a single unselfish act. He had deserted his ship in Greece; he had as readily left the man who befriended him there; he had incurred an obligation with the American who paid his passage to New York, and given no further heed to it; and when arrested for burglary, he had sought to gain a benefit for himself by turning state's evidence against his pal.

"There is no reason why we should give you probation," I said bluntly. "You have not done a single thing to deserve it."

He hung his head; yet even as he did so there was something attractive about him. Given three years of education in place of that period of wanderlust, and he would have made a fine man, with the capacity to rise to leadership in his community.

I left him, and it was several days before I returned. In the meantime, he had replied to his mother's letter, and received an answer in return. There was a mute appeal in his face as he offered it to me; and I still hold it among my papers to-day, a document of supreme importance in this young man's career.

"I have engaged a lawyer to act for you, and I will pay him the costs even if I must sell myself to do it," she wrote. "I cannot let any one know of your disgrace. I cannot explain to others why I no longer sleep or eat when I think of you lying in prison, a young man at the age when life should be full of joy. I wish that I had laid you to rest when you were a baby, Charlie, rather than to have you live for this."

"Your mother is no ordinary woman," I observed, looking up from the reading. "You can't even claim the excuse of a bad home."

"My brothers have both made good," he answered.

But I had not yet come to the burning part of her letter. A moment later I read: "Think of me, Charlie, a girl of twenty, left to the mercy of the world with three little babies. Yet I worked and kept you all, and very often went to the theatre to rehearse without breakfast, so that you should have more. I would say to myself that when my boys grew up they would repay me for all that I had suffered. And what have I to-day? Bertie is out in Africa with a young wife. Frank is a delicate boy, and though he goes to his office each day and is very happy in his work, I fear sometimes that he will never live to see twenty-one. And you!"

"What does she mean when she speaks of going to the theatre to rehearse?" I asked.

"My mother was on the stage at one time. She was very well known, I believe."

I asked him to tell me her stage name, and he did so; and swiftly, as he spoke the words, the walls of the cell faded away, and with it the years, and I was a young man in the balcony of a theatre, loudly joining in the curtain calls for a young dancer who had both London and New York by the ears. Why, there was not a man among us who applauded her grace and beauty who had ever suspected the existence of those three little boys at home, for whose future she danced and sang before the footlights night after night.

Even after all the years the memory of her came back as vividly as though only hours had intervened. I saw again the great audience, leaning forward expectantly; the smiles that greeted her dash on to the stage from the wing; the storm of applause that recalled her. She was joy personified; careless, care-free youth—and the mother of three children, and a widow, all the time!

So that is why I took Charles Tower upon probation,—a young burglar awaiting trial,—and sent him home to his mother. I make this confession now, for he has never returned to this country, and so far as I know, has become such an Englishman as his country has needed so sorely in her days of desperate war.

If you ask me to discuss the ethics of this case, I have nothing to add. There is a phrase often used, "In the judgment of the Court," which implies that a judge must sometimes act at his own discretion, and not be bound too closely by the law as laid down in the Public Statutes. There are times when a probation officer likewise may consider all the circumstances in a case, and act according to the dictates of his own conscience.

It is quite possible that I may have suggested at the time that since Tower was anxious to leave the country, and inasmuch as our corrective experiment with him had not turned out successfully, we would be doing a wise thing for the State and its tax-payers to rid ourselves of him. This was a logical argument, you will admit, and a course justified by the facts in the case.

But what really saved the young man was the appeal of his mother. For the pleasure that she had given me on an evening long ago, when I had supposed her the light-hearted sprite of the world of tinsel and lights, I returned to her the boy who was breaking her heart; the little boy for whom she had gone to the theatre hungry in the days of her professional struggle:—nay more, the child who may have inherited her passion for the applause of the world, though he had translated it into nothing better than the wanderlust.

Life is not such a simple matter after all!

CHAPTER VIII

DRUGS THAT MAKE CRIMINALS OF THEIR VICTIMS

I had been a probation officer less than six months when I made my acquaintance with the first victim of the drug habit. In police circles these unfortunates are known as "dope fiends" or "hops."

It was not until I met Howard Ellis, however, that I began to realize the terrible menace of this widespread evil. Ellis was a college graduate and the son of a distinguished lawyer:—and it is perhaps needless to add that the name I have given him is a fictitious one. His arrest and sentence to the House of Correction for a crime had caused a sensation in the circle of his acquaintances; but the trial had disclosed the fact that he was addicted to a drug, which had been responsible for his downfall.

As was to be expected, strong influences were exerted in his behalf to secure his release upon parole as soon as he had overcome his craving for morphine, and during his weeks of confinement he received every encouragement from the officials of the institution to regain his lost position. The chaplain was especially interested in his case, and was the one who finally interviewed him to prepare the way for his appearance before the Parole

Board. He was given his release, and we all felt the satisfaction of a worthy deed done; when an incident occurred that rather upset our conclusions.

Ellis called upon the chaplain on the following day with a burden upon his mind. He was a gentleman by breeding, and the clergyman sensed that he had come to express his gratitude for what had been done in his behalf, and accordingly sought to dismiss the matter lightly.

"But wait a moment," the young man protested, visibly distressed at the turn the interview was taking. "I want to speak of your visit to me the other day. You came in good faith, and I suppose that you saw nothing strange in my actions at the time."

"Nothing at all," the chaplain replied.

"I ought to tell you, then, that all the time you were talking to me I was considering whether I would kill you. The craving for the drug had returned, and I had become obsessed with the idea that perhaps you had some in your pockets. Had I been sure of this, I would not have hesitated to strangle you, and I want you to know what my condition really is."

I have related this incident merely to illustrate the motive for crime that is to be expected from the secret use of morphine, cocaine, or their several derivatives. Fortunately a Federal law is now in force that is destined to wipe out the illicit traffic in these drugs, and limit their use to the infrequent cases where a registered physician may legitimately prescribe them. But the immediate effect of the enforcement of this law has been to fill the hospitals of the country with drug victims; or if not literally to fill them, at least to appall one with the number of such sufferers. The statistics of this terrible blight upon our civilization are easily obtained, and it is not my purpose to go into them. The discussion in these pages will be limited to certain personal experiences that throw light upon individual cases.

Michael Scullon came before a Massachusetts Court in 1911 charged with breaking and entering on two counts. The evidence against him was, in effect, that he had sought to enter two untenanted buildings in a fashionable suburb of Boston. Such a burglary is unusual, because it is not the work of a professional, and upon the question of sentence several influential Boston men appeared and asked to have the case placed on probation. They said that they knew Scullon, and that he was a vaudeville actor and not a burglar. While they could not account for his escapade, they were willing to vouch for his character, and believed that it would be a grave mistake to imprison him.

My first interview with the man, however, shed a new light upon the matter. His emaciated condition suggested the drug victim; and he confessed when I put the question up to him. "It all came about in this way," he said hopelessly. "I went one night, after the show, to the apartment occupied by the manager of my company. We had not been there long when he and his wife prepared an opium pill and smoked it, and they told me that this was their custom invariably every evening after returning to their rooms. I joined them, because I knew that the drug habit was prevalent among theatrical people, and we are prone to do what our own class does."

I did not take Scullon on probation. His condition did not warrant it, and the Court sent him to the House of Correction for two years, to be placed under the care of the physician there. At the end of eighteen months he had gained twenty pounds, and he was then given his release on parole. During his imprisonment, in the period when he was fighting against the appetite that held him in mental torture for a time, he wrote me a frank and sincere protest against the indiscriminate use of the drug then permitted, and begging the law-makers to enact some legislation that would put a stop to it. I quote briefly from it, as presenting the sort of testimony that did finally induce Congress to act:

"A drug habit is one of the most easily acquired and the hardest to escape from, whether it be cocaine, chloral, morphine or opium. Writing from the standpoint of bitter experience, I venture to assert that if those who make and enforce the laws only had a fair idea of conditions as they really are, laws would be most stringent regarding the sale of all drugs, and more lenient with their victims who run afoul of the law. The young man who becomes an opium smoker is certain to lose his position; but he must still have money to buy the drug. He may commit any offense when undergoing the craving and agony that comes upon him. But the place for him is not a jail or a prison. He should be sentenced to a hospital if he is to be saved. It is not the underworld that chiefly uses drugs. My own experience has shown me from 40 to 60 per cent. of the theatrical profession are addicted to a drug in some form. There are countless drug fiends among society people; and if something is not done for the Negro, a phase of the question that is being quite overlooked, the country will rue his use of cocaine, chloral and laudanum."

Let me submit likewise the written confession of a youth who, at eighteen, had been twice arrested for stealing, and whom I found suffering in a cell in jail: "I went to Boston to find work, and there got in with several young fellows who were using cocaine. In a short time I got so that I would rather have it than my three meals a day. The effects of cocaine are nothing very much except that they make a person feel very good when he is well supplied. But when you cannot get it, you become desperate, and there is nothing that you will hesitate to do to obtain it. At times I would spend the money I had been given for a night's lodging to get 'coke,' and after a time I had to spend from 75 cents to a dollar every day for it. I was in fighting trouble all the time, and when I went three or four days without it I became raving, and my desire was such that there was no crime I would not commit to obtain the necessary money. My moral sense was blunted. I had no sense of right and wrong when I was using it, or in need of it. I am in jail for no other reason than the use of cocaine."

This young man had been a student at an academy for a time, and his written statement is intelligent and prepared with deliberation, affording an important bit of testimony. It required several months to straighten him out, and when he was released, his father did a very sensible thing in sending him to the farm of an uncle in Northern New York, where, with plenty of outdoor work, he was fully restored to physical and mental health.

The efforts of men sent to jail or other institutions, to obtain the drugs to which they have become addicted, are naturally desperate during the early days of their confinement, and the authorities maintain a rigid supervision to prevent the smuggling in of such narcotics. In spite of this watchfulness, however, a "leak" was discovered in one of our Massachusetts corrective institutions,—an experience, it may be added, that other states have had more recently,—and the culprit was finally discovered in the person of one of the minor officers, himself a "dope fiend," as he confessed later. Understanding fully what the craving for morphine was, he had been secretly supplying its victims in their cells, thereby rendering their cure impossible.

He was promptly dismissed from his office and placed under arrest to answer to the charge brought against him, but certain circumstances in the case, notably the fact that his own moral responsibility had been undermined, influenced the Court to place him on probation, and he was given over to my charge. Of course he was both humiliated and repentant, and vowed that he would break the habit that had caused him the loss of his position. I gave him what aid was in my power, and felt confident that he would do as he had promised. Imagine, then, my amazement, to pick up a Sunday newspaper of wide circulation one day and find him "featured" to the extent of a full page with illustrations, as a new Sherlock Holmes, "a man able to point out any criminal or would-be criminal in the surging throng of passersby, one whose study of human characteristics makes his conclusions errorless."

I read the article through to the end with keen enjoyment, because it is not an easy matter to land a Sunday editor with a "pipe dream." This new detector of crime, so the newspaper assured its readers, had made a study of the faces in one of our leading Eastern cities, and had found "a surprising number of bad men, who should be locked up at once before they committed a crime."

There had just occurred in that city a succession of incendiary fires, and this sleuth went on to inform the police that after a study of several hundred known incendiaries, he had been able to establish their type, which was "usually boys or old men with long legs and light bodies." The criminal ear was also marked "below or above the normal size and standing well out of the head," and swindlers were classified as "men having large jaws and prominent cheek bones," differing from pickpockets, who always had "long arms, black hair and scanty beards, and nearly always tall."

There was much more of it, and I could distinguish the haze of morphine through it all. I called the writer to account before the sun set that day, having recognized in him my probationer, and I saw to it that he made no more incursions into literature. Eventually he broke the habit and became a prosperous undertaker, embalming the dead rather than the living.

Only the fringe of this loathsome blight has been touched in the cases that I have cited. One needs but to discover how many thousands of criminals are drug users, and how many tens of thousands of men and women in private life are inefficient through the same slavery, to wonder that the country has so long tolerated the evil. And the pertinent question that arises is as to whether the confirmed drug victim, like the confirmed inebriate, can be cured.

Accepting Massachusetts as a typical state seeking to meet this problem, and we find that the drug victim who voluntarily seeks treatment may obtain it at the State Hospital in Norfolk, a new institution that has not yet reached the limit of its development, or in private hospitals and institutes that are specializing in the work. Dr. Richard C. Cabot, a member of the Harvard Medical School faculty, and a physician of wide experience, has said concerning the treatment of drug victims: "The habit can be cured, but the essential thing is that the patient be a person of backbone, character and stamina. I have seen a woman cured in five days, after using the drug for twenty years. I have seen many physicians treated and cured. On the other hand, I have had persons dragged to me by their relatives for treatment who did not have the character to resist temptation after they returned to their environment."

This is a statement complete and final. The majority of drug victims were not being saved prior to the enforcement of the Federal law because they returned to an environment where temptation still awaited them. It was only when the suppression of the traffic reached the point where drugs were to be obtained only with difficulty, and often at exhorbitant prices, that confirmed users found themselves in desperate straits, and gave the matter of their cure serious thought.

At Norfolk during the past few months more men have applied for drug treatment than for a cure from alcoholism, though the hospital was established primarily for the inebriates. Many give themselves up voluntarily; others have been gathered in by the police and sent there against their will. In the latter cases a rigid search is necessary, for many of these men anticipated the stringency in the drug market, and cleverly provided against it. The contraband is sometimes found concealed in a shoulder pad; in a shoe; in the lining of a hat. One victim, amply supplied with money, had invested a thousand dollars in his favorite drug, all intended for his own consumption.

There is no mystery shrouding the treatment at this State Hospital. The patient is given his drug in diminishing doses, lest the sudden cutting off of it bring about a too great mental reaction; and then he is sent into the open air to work, receiving from time to time mental suggestions as to his ability to conquer the craving by his own will. In time he is released, theoretically cured; but whether his relief is permanent depends upon his own determination never to touch a drug again.

The work of the Government is by no means ended in this great crusade. Until the last of the vast number of victims is dead or cured, there will exist the temptation to supply the half-crazed men and women with a drug or its substitute. Already patients are appearing in hospitals suffering from an improper use of Dover's powders, ordinarily employed in the treatment of fevers, and from ergot, a little known drug that promises to become fatal in its effects. Given to a rooster experimentally, ergot causes the blood in the comb to coagulate until it sometimes falls off; and one may expect that men who undertake to use it regularly will finish abruptly with sudden death.

The treatment of drug users in certain of the private hospitals that require a high fee, but claim a large percentage of permanent cures, extends from a few days to three weeks. Mental suggestion and an appeal to the will-power of the patient are employed, but more reliance is placed upon a substitute for the drug. Frequently the person under treatment believes that the drug is still being administered, only to learn that it has been discontinued for several days without his knowledge.

The criminal who is addicted to a drug,—and who may have become a criminal only after he became a "hop,"—oftentimes finds himself in great mental anguish when his supply is suddenly cut short by arrest. In the more enlightened states, where the medical phase of the problem is better understood, such a prisoner is given the special treatment that he requires, and very little is expected from him until he is physically restored. It is not the punishment of the law that such men merit, but an enlightening as to the insidious action of the drugs upon them, and the final death that inevitably awaits them if they return to the practice. For the majority of men who fall to this state are completely ignorant in medical matters.

Occasionally one finds among these drug victims in the cells the man who comes to a personal realization of his danger, and makes his fight alone to avert it. A chaplain in one of our Massachusetts prisons told me the story that follows.

An elderly man awaiting trial sent him an urgent message from his cell, requesting an interview with him, and the clergyman responded to find a face so terribly marked with vice and depravity that he shrank from entering, familiar as he was with prison sights.

"I do not care to talk about the crime that I have committed," said the prisoner by way of explanation. "I am willing to take any sentence that the Court imposes, but I want to make a confession of another kind."

He broke down at this point and wept, completely unnerved. The chaplain told me that he never saw a man give way to such emotion, and his tears literally fell upon the stone pavement.

"My parents were thrifty, honest New Englanders," he said at length. "They had means, and were liberal in bringing me up. I went to an academy and to college, and had every opportunity to become a useful man. I loved the company of good women; I was fond of flowers; and only the cleanest and best books appealed to me. There was nothing vicious in my nature, and when the Civil War came on, I enlisted from a sense of patriotism. At one time during the war I served on the body guard of Abraham Lincoln.

"But I left the army with the opium habit fastened upon me, and it has held me in its power ever since. I fought to free the slaves, but for all these years I have been serving a master no less cruel. I live only to smoke the pipe and gain the degraded visions that come from it. My mind is a human cesspool. I cannot describe its horrors, and I have become a dangerous criminal because I have no other object than to get the drug. I have sent for you because you are the chaplain. Look into the hell of opium where my soul lives, and tell me whether you can give me any hope before I die."

The chaplain looked into the piteous face of this old man, and realized that all his own faith was put to the test.

"There is hope for you only through yourself

and God," he replied. "The State will protect you from the drug, but it is between you and God to conquer the appetite."

They talked the matter over at some length, very seriously and with no evasions. The aged prisoner knew what terrors he must face when the recurring longing for the drug came upon him, but he agreed to make the fight against it.

The day of his trial came, and against the unanswerable evidence that the prosecuting attorney offered, he made no protest. A sentence of fifteen years in prison was imposed upon him, and he passed out of the court room to end his life in a cell.

It was four years before the chaplain saw him again; and then, walking through the prison one day, a voice addressed him from one of the cells. He paused, but did not recognize the face of the man who spoke, for his own duties had kept him at another institution during the interval.

"I am the man you saved," he said. "I am the happiest man in prison."

His face had changed from all resemblance to the man who had appealed to him from the depths of his degradation.

"I remember," said the chaplain. "You are the man who made the fight against opium. So you won?"

"By the grace of God," replied the smiling prisoner.

CHAPTER IX

THE TRAIL OF CRIME IN THE WAKE OF THE LIQUOR TRAFFIC

One may consider the liquor traffic and its effect upon human life from as many angles as war is viewed. The most ardent peace advocates are the men who have never served in the army; and the greatest foes of alcohol are the men and women who do not use it. Then there are those who believe that war is necessary to national expansion, and that the licensed saloon in a city promotes business; while others hold that warfare brutalizes the manhood of a nation, and liquor debauches all who touch it.

But the man who views a battlefield at close range sweeps all theories of war aside when confronted by the fact of its dreadful carnage. He realizes for the first time the inefficiency and waste of a system that takes men from peaceful, productive life, and in a brief hour leaves them mangled or dead; that destroys industries, ruins towns, dynamites bridges, wrecks homes. And so it is with this liquor traffic. You may have held any inherited theory concerning its proper control, the right of the state to interfere with a man's personal liberty, the folly of attempting to extinguish an appetite as old as civilization; but all are forgotten when you come upon the actual havoc wrought by the business—the men hurried to untimely graves, the men sent to prison for crimes committed under the influence of liquor, the women and children reduced to extreme poverty, the homes broken up, the business careers ruined.

When first I became a probation officer, there were a great many things concerning the source of crime that I had yet to learn from experience. I had not seen what really became of the prisoners at the bar after sentence had been imposed upon them; and when, soon after my appointment, I was invited to witness the execution of a murderer, I accepted with keen interest. It was before the adoption of electrocution for the death penalty, when condemned men were still sentenced "to be hanged by the neck until dead." The prisoner who was to go to his death in this manner had been convicted of killing an old man to cover a petty robbery. The crime had been brutal, and without mitigating circumstance.

It was a poor, ignorant man thus going to his grave, unmarried and friendless, but his last scene had been staged with the traditional dignity of the state. We assembled in the drawing-room of the keeper of the jail, a small group of sober-faced men, and marched with decorum to the long corridor where chairs had been provided directly in front of the grim, skeleton-looking scaffold. The deputy sheriffs, in their frock coats, white gloves and silk hats, arranged the final details, and then the sheriff of the county entered, bearing in his hand his wand of office, and leading a small procession, in the midst of which was the condemned man.

The murderer stepped upon the trapdoor of the scaffold, the least concerned of all those present, and the straps were adjusted to his arms and legs. Then the sheriff spoke as the law required of him, saying: "The time has arrived when the fell sentence of the law must be carried out, and if you have anything to say, or any parting message to give, the last and only opportunity is at hand."

There was complete silence for a moment, and we listened intently, for at the trial the defendant had protested his innocence, and had gone upon the witness stand in an effort to prove that the crime had been committed by a tramp just prior to his discovery of the body.

Facing us, with the black cap that would shut out forever the light of day and the face of his fellow men, ready to be drawn, the condemned man calmly and deliberately uttered these words: "Dear friends, never go into a saloon. Never drink another drop of liquor, for if you do you will repent of it sooner or later. It may lead you, as it has me, to the gallows."

The cap was adjusted; the trap fell; a struggling body gave up its spirit, and another life was added to the toll of rum within our Commonwealth. We walked away softly, none of us having enjoyed the spectacle, and I thought over just what that man's confession meant. He had worked on a farm for small wages, and his one failing was an occasional spree when he received his money and went to the city. The thirst had caught him one day when he had spent his savings, and he had committed murder to secure a few dollars to satisfy his craving. Did the blame for the crime rest solely upon him, or did the man who sold liquor and the State that legalized it also share in the responsibility?

I went from that scene, not rabid against the licensed saloon, but sober in my desire to study its effects more closely. It had become my duty to aid men and women in difficulty with the courts, and to do this intelligently I must trace crime of every sort back to its beginning, and consider all its circumstances. I was aware, with the average citizen, that the great bulk of our poverty and crime was to be laid at the door of the saloon-keeper and the dealer in bottled liquors, but my information was general rather than specific. I opened my mind now to every bit of evidence that came before me bearing upon the liquor question.

In court we often listen to the testimony of the

expert witness. He is the man with a scientific knowledge of his subject, and judge and jury give weight to what he says, because his opinion is based upon study and experiment, and not influenced by partisan feeling. I very soon discovered that a great many experts were testifying against the liquor traffic, though very little heed was being given to what they said.

Dr. T. D. Crothers was one of them. Within a period of six months he had found six homicides sentenced to death who had been using spirits to excess before committing their crime, and he had written in comment:

"To assume sanity in any person who persists in using spirits to excess, a habit destructive to all his personal and pecuniary interests, is contrary to facts, and is simply the tenacity of an old delusion of the value of alcohol. From clinical facts and teachings I affirm with confidence that no one who uses spirits to excess for any length of time has a normal, sound brain. It is a delusion to consider that all inebriates have the power to drink and abstain at will; that intoxication implies a voluntary state which is under control of the mind."

How often has the truth of this statement been checked up in my own experience since I read those words! It is not crime alone that one finds in the wake of intemperance, but the threatened tragedies in the homes, concerning which the public almost never hears.

I was summoned one night to a home in one of the best residential quarters of a city. The probation officer's work is not limited to the cases placed in his hands by the Court, nor are his working hours confined to the day itself; and when this message came over the telephone, I knew it to be one of those unofficial appeals from a stricken home supposed to be above reproach.

So I hurried to the address given, and there I found in bed, in the best favored room of the house, an attractive man still under thirty-five, with some stamp of dissipation upon his face, but yet not so marred but that one would protest against a person of his position in life going to the devil so readily. He held an important salaried position, and he had been drinking for a year. The habit had fastened itself upon him from the stages of after-dinner drinking, before-meals drinking, and an occasional all-night spree, to his present condition, where he was content to lie in bed and keep himself partially stupefied with whiskey.

He had forgotten his business. He had forgotten the mother who had remained by him for a week, seeking in vain to sober him off. He would get up only when his secret supply of liquor was running low, and armed with a revolver he would dress and go for more, returning to his bed again as soon as he had obtained it. Naturally the family feared that the ultimate outcome would be either murder or suicide.

It was a desperate case, but not a new one to me. The saloon and the brothel do not claim all the victims, for I have often found them in the reputable club, and in such homes as this. I sat down by the bed and began to talk as man to man to this young drunkard in his silk pajamas. I knew the position that he held, and what was expected of him in life, but most of all I understood the agony of his mother.

"Oh, it's no use," he told me as I argued with him. "I'm too far gone."

Still I talked; and finally he appeared to come to his senses, for he gave me his pledge that he would quit where he was, and never touch liquor again.

But Crothers is right in saying that no one who uses spirits for any length of time has a normal, sound brain. I returned on the following night and found him stupidly drunk. He had given up his bottle of liquor on the preceding evening, and had arisen in the morning with the avowed purpose of pulling himself together and getting back to his office; but here he was, as bad off as before.

"Well, that young man will never be brought to his senses without a shock of some kind, and I think that it can be done without incurring much publicity," I advised his parents.

They told me to do whatever I thought best with him, and I went to the telephone and had a confidential talk with the night captain at police headquarters.

At an hour when respectable people had gone to their homes, a discreet police inspector called at the house with a taxicab and entered the young man's room. We secured the loaded revolver, and then we exchanged the silken pajamas for a suit of clothes, and we informed the occupant of the room that he was under arrest.

He was derisive at first; angry when we bundled him into the waiting taxi; alarmed when we locked him up in a cell for the night. It was an indignity to which he had never before been subjected.

We allowed him to remain there in doubt as to what would happen to him until after the regular session of the Court on the following morning; but just before the judge retired to his room we took him before the Court and had him remanded to the county jail for ten days. My plan was to arouse him from his mental torpor and then send him to an institution for special treatment. It succeeded in a measure, for he became so enraged when he found himself in jail that he sent for the keeper, demanded his rights as an American citizen, and actually gained permission to go to the telephone.

There he made the wires hot in an effort to obtain bondsmen and regain his freedom, and it was not long before he had convinced a number of people that he was the victim of a conspiracy. By the time he did obtain his release,—and he was not let out that day,—he showed no signs of the liquor, and returned to his business with every outward indication that a great wrong had been done to him.

His business associates were glad to see him back again, and matters that had been waiting his attention called him at once to another state. And almost immediately his family received telegraphic information that he had broken out again, and it became necessary to send a relative for him to save him from arrest.

There was no question now as to what our rights were in the matter. He was promptly examined by two physicians, adjudged to be a dipsomaniac, and sent to the State Hospital at Norfolk for treatment.

This hospital is the official recognition in Massachusetts of the fact that drunkenness is less a crime than a disease. Dr. Irwin H. Neff, its capable head, said in addressing a meeting of the American Medico-Psychological Association: "The medical profession has been singularly lacking in an appreciation of the fact that the problem of the amelioration of this condition (the liquor problem) is within its province. Sociologists, philanthropists and jurists have for years struggled with the question and have failed to arrive at any satisfactory solution. One of the greatest difficulties that the medical man has to overcome is the need of convincing the public that the many alleged cures for drunkenness now existing are not countenanced by the medical profession, but are the product of a successful system of quackery which has flourished profitably for years."

To this institution we sent our dipsomaniac; not a hospital in the commonly accepted sense, but an estate of a thousand acres far from a city, set among the hills, and affording abundant opportunity for physical labor. "Good physical health is the foundation upon which the cure of habitual drunkenness must be built," says Dr. Neff; and work and rest are so arranged as to habituate the patient to regularity, for inebriates are characteristically persons of irregular habits, and the creation of order in their lives serves to reduce temptation and to provide the basis for moral living. A type of work is chosen for each patient congenial to him; "for," to quote Dr. Neff again, "successful curative treatment of inebriety is not medical in any narrow sense, but it is mental. There is no known specific. Cures are accomplished through suggestion, not drugs. The hospital alone, of all state institutions, can provide those elements of suggestion and moral suasion that constitute a large part of psychotherapy. The coöperation of the patient, so necessary as a condition of success in the treatment by mental suggestion, can not readily be elicited in the prison, where discipline and restraint tend to arouse antagonism."

Let me dismiss my dipsomaniac to pass on to the larger question involved in the statement that I have quoted. He was discharged at the end of the month, and has since refrained from the use of liquor. We have the right to assume that his cure is permanent.

But such cases as this do not constitute the real problem of drunkenness. What of our treatment of the countless host of men who stagger along our public streets, and whose arrest is so often necessary in the interest of the public peace? G. E. Partridge, in his "Studies in the Psychology of Intemperance," has said: "What could be more wrong than to try to cure the drunkard by punishment and isolation, whose greatest need is a normal social life? It is not to be wondered at that our officials who administer justice almost invariably believe the drunkard incurable."

And this is likewise a statement quite true. From the very beginning of our Colonial period we Americans have had this problem before us in some form and only recently have we shown any real intelligence in dealing with it. You may turn back in the old records to-day and find where, in September of 1633, Robert Coles was fined four shillings and "enjoined to stand with a white sheet of paper on his back, whereon the words 'A Drunkard' shall be written in great letters, and to stand therewith so long as the Court thinks mete, for abusing himself with drink." That was the period when England was seeking to reform drunkards by compelling them to wear an inverted barrel with holes cut for the head and hands. The barrel and the paper placard failing to assure reform, the stocks and the "bilboes" were tried with no better success.

If probation has accomplished nothing more, it has justified itself by the service that it has performed to the intoxicated man and his family. It has not solved the problem,—one must strike directly at the root of the evil to accomplish that,—but at least it has rescued the salvage from among the drunkards.

Prior to the year 1901 we punished inebriety as a crime, and almost without intelligent discrimination. For example, in a single year 20,151 persons were sent to jail for drunkenness in Massachusetts, although the courts had ordered the imprisonment of only 8411 of the number! The other 11,740 had been fined, but being unable to produce the few dollars assessed against them as the price of their return to liberty and the work awaiting them in the majority of cases, had been caught in the claws of the law that sent them to the common jail if the fine was not paid.

Those of us who are in comfortable circumstances would have no difficulty in finding a friend willing to loan us two or three dollars upon request; but the man just convicted of drunkenness, who must hire

a court messenger to summon his friends to come to
his aid unless a faithful wife or sister missed him
overnight, often found the fine a complete barrier
against the freedom offered to him.   Hundreds of
thousands of men went to jail in the years while this
law was in force in various states, and for the time
being became unproductive, and added to the burden of the taxpayers.

The more intelligent treatment of the drunkard
has now been adopted in the leading states of the
country.   The occasional offender is sent home without an appearance in court for his first and second
arrest within a year, and even after that he may be
placed upon probation if there is a chance to save
him.   And in cases where a fine is imposed, the defendant is given a reasonable time to pay it through
the probation office, if his bout of drinking has left
him without money for the time being.   This more
generous treatment has not resulted in an increase
of intemperance, and it has decreased the number of
men who are lost for a time to their regular occupation, since they continue to support their families
while on probation; and not infrequently with much
better success than during the period preceding their
arrest.

As a more charitable world now views the problem, the inebriate, like the victim of drugs, has contracted a disease; wilfully, to be sure, since he had
full information upon the subject, but requiring

treatment rather than punishment.   This is the only phase of the problem with which my office deals, and there is no remedy that the probation officer does not try out in the course of his experience.   Certain well-defined diseases will yield to recognized treatment, but intemperance in its advanced stages is not so easily conquered.

I have employed every expedient that came to hand in an effort to save men in bondage to the saloons.   I compelled one man, before I would accept him upon probation for drunkenness, to agree to attend church every Sunday for a year, his clergyman to report to me regularly.   He had not been an attendant for years, but the church came to his support, and he kept his pledge.

There is a policeman upon a beat in one of our cities whose career hung by a thread a few years ago.   He was about to be dishonorably discharged, when I argued with his superiors that his complete downfall was inevitable in that event, and that if he was worth saving, it must be done in some other manner.   We sent him to an institute that treated such cases.   It was not always successful in permanently curing drunkenness, but in this case it did not fail.

Again, there was a man who had studied for the clergy, and who, to the humiliation of his friends, became a sot instead.   He had a record of thirty convictions for drunkenness before his people finally saw him in the light of a dipsomaniac, in need of medical treatment rather than police regulation. That was three years ago, and he has been a total abstainer ever since.

A woman came to me to recommend a discreet lawyer who would secure for her a divorce on the grounds of confirmed habits of intoxication.

"Have you the money to pay a lawyer?" I inquired.

"I have," she answered.

"Would you divorce your husband upon any other grounds?"

"No, indeed," she replied. "He is the best fellow in the world when sober."

"Then why not spend the divorce money to give him one more chance through medical treatment?" I suggested.

She did so, although her husband was in jail at the time, awaiting trial on an appeal from the lower court. His release was obtained when the somewhat unusual circumstances of the case were made clear, and he was placed in the hands of a specialist for three days. That was in 1911, and he has not tasted liquor since that time. When a commission in Massachusetts began its investigation of drunkenness, he voluntarily appeared before it as a witness.

It is my purpose in citing these cases to offer hope to those countless families afflicted with a drunken husband or son. There is no need to discuss with them the ethics of the liquor traffic; what they desire to know is whether the curse can be lifted from their own doorposts.

A woman's voice at the telephone called me one night to a home of ample means, and a family above reproach. I had no knowledge of a skeleton in the family closet there, and was at my wits' end to know what could have happened when I found the various members assembled in the living-room. Yet their faces betrayed the fact that some calamity had fallen upon the household.

The father, a man holding a position of responsibility over hundreds of employees, led me to the kitchen, and with bowed head introduced me to his maudlin, eldest son, a prodigal who had returned after an absence of many months, and whose name was never mentioned among the family's friends. The sight of the son at the door that night had caused the father to fall in a swoon, and had prompted the mother to call for aid. For years this had been the traditional black sheep of the family, returning periodically at the end of some riotous spree to demand money as the price of his leaving the town.

The father's grief was so apparent that I sent him from the room, and even the son was vaguely touched by it, and reproached himself for always seeking out his home at such a time.

"Why don't you cut it out?" I demanded, with unconcealed contempt in my voice.

"I've been a sport, and I am beyond redemption," he answered; and pulling himself together, gave me a recital of some of his experiences in the world. It was not a pleasant story.

"It is a short life, but a merry one," he concluded. "I am already a doomed man."

"If you mean that you are going to drink yourself to death, that is pure rot," I said. "You can be cured of the drink habit."

He laughed without mirth. "I've tried the cures," he said. "I've been to the farm colonies and all that sort of thing, and you see where I am."

"I will lay you a wager that I can stop you drinking in twenty-four hours," I said with conviction. "And I will bet you twenty dollars to your one."

"Nonsense!" he answered. "It can't be done."

The effort to keep up the conversation was becoming a tax upon his muddled brain, and his manner indicated that he desired to be rid of me. I concluded that I had better get after him more vigorously.

"You have been talking about being a sport, but you're a pretty poor one after all," I remarked ironically. "You'll take my offer, or you will take the worst thrashing you ever had in your life."

He sat up at this. "Who are you, anyway?" he demanded.

"Never mind, but I will keep my word," I replied.

"Twenty to one," said he thoughtfully. "And you've got to stop me in twenty-four hours. I'll take you."

"This seems to be a case for private treatment," I said to his father, talking the matter over with him later. "He has been given farm treatment as an inebriate, and has not responded to suggestion. We've got to drive the thing out of him."

The father gave me authority to act as I deemed wise, and did not limit me as to expenditures.

Let me state here that while I agree with Dr. Neff that the majority of so-called "cures" for drunkenness are not successful, I do not debar all private hospitals and institutes. An Australian Commission, sent to the United States in 1910 to gain light upon this problem, found one method of treatment that had a record of 60 per cent. of cures, and recommended it for Government use in Australia. It is now in use there free of charge. Our own commissions have not gone so far, and the treatment remains in private hands, too costly to be within the reach of poor men.

Since my own work is essentially practical, and 60 per cent. is a working average, I had sent a number of paying patients to this treatment, and the results seemed to justify a similar course in the present instance.

I was at the railroad station by appointment on the following morning, but I did not see the other party to my wager. A member of the family greeted me and told me with some chagrin how the prodigal was in hiding somewhere about the station, having taken to cover upon my approach. I relate this circumstance as disclosing the mental condition into which a once strong man may lapse after he has become a victim of alcohol. As Crothers has said, to assume full sanity in such a case is to acknowledge the tenacity of an old delusion.

Eventually we landed him in Boston on a later train, and a carriage took us to one of the quiet residential streets, where we found a private hospital with no mark to distinguish it from the other dwellings.

The manager and the physician were introduced to the new patient, and he confided to them the joke of my proposed redemption of him. Possibly he would have been less humorously inclined had he known that the man just obtaining his discharge as we entered was a prosperous liquor dealer, who had paid a good fee to be saved from his own goods. As it was, the physician lifted his eyebrows to me, and asked my companion what he would have to drink.

"What have you got?" inquired the prodigal cordially.

"Anything from beer to champagne," replied the doctor.

"Make it a sandwich and a high ball," the prodigal ordered piously. "I like to take food with my drink."

They conducted him to a large, pleasant room, with a servant in white to wait upon him. This servant was a graduate nurse, though the prodigal was not aware of the fact. He was more interested in the magazines and books at hand, the bountiful supply of good tobacco and the funny stories that the doctor told whenever he dropped in for a friendly call.

At dinner the prodigal ate roast beef, vegetables, drank a bottle of beer, and was given his first wine glass of medicine. A quarter of an hour later he inquired as to whether another drink would be permitted. "We have them on tap all the time," the servant replied. "Order whenever you like."

He selected his liquor, but it did not taste quite right, a fact that he attributed to his having eaten too much dinner. At supper time when offered liquor, he declined. His appetite for food was likewise lacking.

"No wonder," he observed. "I've been hitting too fast a pace lately, and need sleep." So he retired early.

His slumbers that night were troubled, and he had no appetite in the morning. The young man in white offered him grape fruit, cereal, chops and coffee; but he said that what he really needed was a drink.   Liquor was brought to him, but he pushed the glass away.   He even selected the goblet containing his medicine in preference.   Although he did not know it, he was through with alcoholic drinks, and I had won my wager.

I saw him two days later.   If ever there was a regenerated man, here was one, though he still had a day to go with the treatment.   His appetite had begun to return and he could look at himself rationally, and was beginning to think seriously of his own affairs.   On the third day they insisted that he drink a glass of beer, and it made him so ill that he would not even look at a liquor bottle after that.

He returned to his father's home, and asked to be permitted to remain there.   He went to work, and to-day, after an interval of three years, he is successful in his business, married very happily, interested in a Y. M. C. A. and an active member of a church.

What is the last stage from which a drunkard can be rescued?   I do not know; but I have the record of Thomas Hanks, whom I sent to an institution for medical treatment in 1912.   He had been arrested forty times for drunkenness, and our various corrective institutions had tried their best to check him, but in vain.   He seemed to be on the direct road to a drunkard's grave; yet he responded to treatment, and is a sober, self-respecting citizen today. Moreover, he is one of those who see in national prohibition the only wholesale cure for the evil. He has been to the very root of the matter, and realizes that while we saved him, a hundred others, less fortunate, were lost. The economic side of the question has come to have an appeal for him. For years his efficiency was wasted, and he finds himself now without the resources, financial or social, that a man should have in middle life. If the Government has seen fit to suppress drugs, he sees no reason why, in due time, it will not also cut out booze. That is his idea of getting at the root of the traffic.

And what would it mean to the administration of justice if this evil could be completely abolished? Of the 176,618 arrests in Massachusetts in 1914, 70 per cent. were for drunkenness! It was a new flood-tide mark for inebriety, in spite of all that we had done to check it.

CHAPTER X

The man who sat in my office at the Court House glowered at me with the aroused instincts of a citizen who believes that his personal rights have been violated. It was early June, and in the trees outside the birds were still mating, and their twitterings came in through the open windows. Our conversation, however, had reached the point where such soft sounds were unnoticed.

"Have I broken any law?" he demanded. "What do you mean by threatening me with arrest? You've got the wrong man. I'll not stand for it."

"Be reasonable," I said quietly, for one becomes accustomed to blustering citizens. "Nobody has threatened you. I am merely telling you what may happen, as a matter of fact, if you don't support your wife and family."

"You make me tired!" he declared ironically. A citizen who believes himself to be within his rights will not accept uninvited advice from anybody. "Don't you suppose that I know that the divorce court was in session in this very building for two weeks, dealing with just such cases as mine? Did you cause the arrest of any of the parties in those cases? Well, I guess not! They had lawyers. I prefer to manage my own affairs; and you order me to come to your office and then you try to tell me what I will do in my own family."

"Now we are getting somewhere," I said. "So you intend to divorce your wife and two small children. You have found an affinity, I suppose."

His eyes blazed, but not before they assured me that there was another woman in his domestic triangle. From what I had learned concerning him before he accepted my invitation to an interview, I recognized in him just the plain, average man. His education had been limited. His income from a trade was $18 a week. He was something of a dandy in a small way in personal appearance, and a noticeable contrast to the tired, discouraged little woman who had come to me with her troubles, seeking to avert publicity if possible. He had left her six weeks before, after a quarrel, with the statement that he was through with her and would never return, and the struggle to support herself and the children during that brief period had quite convinced her that she could not make it go without him. I had thought that a fair measure of the blame might rest with her, since the woman who becomes indifferent to her personal appearance often fails to hold the interest of her husband in a home of this class, but the discovery of the other woman as a factor shifted the responsibility to the man. He had not only become tired of his wife, but he proposed to divorce her and marry another.

"If your wife wanted a divorce, she might obtain it in time on the ground of desertion, but I do not understand that she seeks it," I said.

"I am tired of the whole business," he complained. "We don't pull together, and I have about decided to quit the state and have done with her. You can tell her if you want to."

"Going to Nevada?" I inquired.

"Who told you that?" he asked suspiciously.

"Nobody; but husbands frequently do. The district attorney sent an officer out there only last month to bring back a man who had done that very thing. It might pay you to consult the district attorney before leaving Massachusetts. He has made a specialty of non-support cases, and you would be interested in his point of view."

"Do you mean to say that a citizen of Massachusetts hasn't a right to go to Nevada to get a divorce from his wife?" he demanded angrily. "How long has that fool law been on the statute books?"

"The Uniform Desertion Act became a law in 1911, but has since been amended and improved," I answered. "But you miss the whole point in the matter. If your wife had become unfaithful to you, or had contracted confirmed habits of intoxication, or for other sufficient reasons unfitted herself to remain your wife and the mother of your children, then you would have the usual appeal to the law, and we would have nothing to say in your affairs.   But you can not break the marriage vows just because you happen to tire of them.   You have signed a legal and binding contract, and the Commonwealth proposes that you shall live up to it. Let me show you."

I opened my Manual of Laws, compiled for probation officers, and read aloud: "Any husband who without just cause deserts his wife or minor child or children, whether by going into another town or city in this Commonwealth, or into another state, and leaves them without making reasonable provision for their support, shall be guilty of a crime, and on conviction shall be punished by a fine or by imprisonment, or by both."

"Has she complained against me?" he asked with a dangerous gleam in his eyes.

"No, and she will not do so," I replied.

"Ah!" said he, and prepared to end the interview.

"One moment more," I begged.   "The law further provides that complaint may be made by any citizen or by an officer.   The district attorney can cause your arrest.   So can I."

"Go ahead," he said.   "Arrest me, and I'll pay the fine, and what do any of you get out of it then?"

"You are still thinking of the old law," I said politely.   "It is true that the money would have gone

to the county, or if you had been imprisoned your
family would not have been benefited by it.   Now
it is quite different.   The Court may fine you $200,
and the money will be paid over to me, to be made
over to your wife and children on a weekly allowance, your arrest to follow again if you still disobey the law.   Or if you are unable to pay the fine,
and prefer to be sent to the House of Correction, I
shall be able to collect fifty cents a day for your
labor from the master of the institution as long as
you remain there.   It is likely, however, that if arrested I shall ask the Court to place you on probation, with the agreement that you return to work
and pay over to me for the support of your family
a stated sum each week for an indefinite period.   I
have almost a hundred men on probation under
these terms at the present time."

At this he wilted and capitulated.   As I have
stated, he was only the average man, and the fact
had escaped him that we had been legislating to
provide justice for the woman and her children in
just such cases as his own.   I was sorry for him,
because it is not an easy matter to mend these
broken homes, and while the husband was in the
wrong now, there must have been some failure on
the woman's part in the beginning.   About all that
I could seek was justice for the children, who were
in no wise to blame for the failures of their parents.

Before long we were discussing his troubles with

less animosity, and I took occasion to relate to him some of my experiences in dealing with men arrested for non-support, and later placed on probation. The statutes provide for the payment of a weekly sum to the wife for a period of two years, but I told him that in practice I required it indefinitely, or as long as the couple continued to live apart, so that much unhappiness was to be avoided by patching up the misunderstanding in the beginning. I related to him the case of one man now living in Vermont, who is required to send six dollars a week to his wife and children in California. They have drifted far apart since the day of his arrest, but the obligation still rests upon him. I was collecting money in Massachusetts and paying it in Ireland; in New York and sending it on to Canada.

I recalled another case in which a man had been indicted while hiding in Rhode Island. He had been hunted down and brought back, and I had taken him on probation with an agreement to contribute $3 a week to the support of his family; but after a few payments he and his wife had become reconciled, and had gone to re-establish their home in a city where they were unknown.

The end of our discussion was the promise of the man in my office to perform voluntarily the duty that the law could have compelled, and he left me in quite a different frame of mind from that in which he had entered.

I have related this incident because it introduces an important new field in which probation officers may work in the states that have adopted this enlightened legislation. The matter may well commend itself to the attention of governors in those states that are still backward in framing laws for the protection of women and children.

Massachusetts probation officers in 1915 collected and paid over to the support of deserted wives and children the sum of $219,984, and since the cost of maintaining the entire probation system was $148,000, this single branch of the work more than justified the outlay. Needless to observe, a large number of these women and children would have come upon their community for support had the husband escaped his responsibility.

Another important step has been taken in behalf of the unfortunate young women who become mothers without the protection of marriage. New England laws have been strictly enforced against physicians who sought to relieve this vexing problem of the deceived or wayward girl, but only recently has the responsibility been placed where it really belongs, upon the father of the child.

In my own experience I had often found in jail, apparently overlooked or forgotten, the man whose arrest had been caused by the woman he had betrayed; and if I venture to discuss a topic so often excluded from polite society, it is because we have too long ignored the matter through prudery or moral cowardice.

In the first terror at the discovery of her position, the woman, failing to obtain a promise of speedy marriage, would cause the man's arrest, and frequently he would be unable to obtain bail, and as often had no lawyer to look after his interests. The girl, on her part, left the matter to the routine of the courts, having no legal adviser, and so four or five months might elapse before the birth of the child and the trial of the case. The defendant would then plead guilty, and if inclined to escape further liability, believing himself sufficiently punished, had only to take the poor debtor's oath, and after remaining in jail for thirty days more, finally go free, having done nothing for his child, but having deteriorated mentally during his confinement.

With a knowledge of these facts, I petitioned the Massachusetts Legislature in 1913 to have these cases placed under the law governing non-support, and a measure to this effect was enacted. We have not been able to reach the root of the problem, for the same succession of these unfortunate cases continues; but we have at least put the matter upon a fairer basis. When the man is arrested now, he is placed on probation and compelled to contribute to the support of his offspring; and as this fact becomes more widely known, it may serve, in some measure at least, to check the passions of men who too lightly regard the womanhood of their land.

It must not be assumed, however, that probation in the cases grouped in this chapter is merely a matter of routine in the probation office.   As a matter of fact, an entirely new class has been developed for treatment, since the men brought to book do not always consider themselves de facto offenders against the law, and consequently are often prone to accept probation as an opportunity to escape from serious punishment.   My experience with a man who may be known as John Doe for the purposes of this narrative will serve to illustrate just how much work may be involved in one of these cases.

Mrs. Doe had not received support from her husband for several years when she learned one day of the change in the Massachusetts law, and had a warrant issued for his arrest.   In her long struggle to keep her children sheltered and fed, she had become embittered, and no longer cherished affection for the man who had deserted her, but when chance provided her with the clue as to his whereabouts, and she learned that he was in comfortable circumstances, the unfairness of the situation swept over her, and she desired that the law exact the last dollar that was lawfully hers.

The authorities brought John Doe back from another state, and in his trail came a woman very much interested in him, and conspicuous to me, at least, by her attendance at his trial. The man was found guilty, and the question arose as to whether he should be given probation, or sent to the House of Correction. He was quite frank in telling me that he had established himself elsewhere, and no longer cared for his wife or children. The former had been responsible for his leaving home, he said, and she had shown herself able to maintain her family during the several years of their separation, which he considered a matter of mutual agreement.

"Nevertheless you are responsible for your children," I told him. "You have shirked the liability all this time, and now you must meet it or I will refuse to accept you on probation, and you will be sent away, which is an alternative that a man with your ability to earn wages should not face."

He agreed that this was so, for he had never been arrested before, and the personal humiliation involved appealed to him where the dependence of his children failed to touch him.

I therefore accepted his promise to make regular payments, and he was released on probation; but the first week passed, and the second likewise, and no money was paid over to me for the support of his minor children.

It has been my purpose in these pages to make clear the fact that while probation is easily obtained where the circumstances seem to warrant it, its requirements must be respected; and as in the case of Thomas Dulan I was willing to go any length to put my hands upon him again, so now, I determined to have John Doe back in court if it required all the resources of the county to apprehend him. It was before I had learned by experience that it is wisdom to require a cash bond or a joint surety in such cases. Nowadays a John Doe, if I am suspicious of him, must deposit the equivalent of $500 as a proof that his word is quite as good as his bond. But this was one of my first cases, and having no financial hold upon him, I must bring him back or admit myself hoodwinked.

Unfortunately I did not know where he had gone, and I was not inclined to report the matter to the regular police and thereby admit my own credulity in the matter. I started out alone in search of a clue.

Now I am in no sense a detective. My peculiar profession requires that I should be as far removed from the traditional police officer as possible, since their professional point of view is known to the men whom they are called upon to arrest. But I went about the task as best I could.

During the consideration of the case in court I had obtained possession of a few facts concerning John Doe. He had an aged mother who looked askance at the woman who had come to town with him, and I had learned that the latter came from Hartford, Connecticut. I began to construct my pursuit of him by assuming that he was probably living with this woman as his wife, and since she had disappeared after the trial, that he had gone somewhere to join her. What more likely city than Hartford?

To Hartford I went, and consulting a directory, learned that there was but one family in the city of the same name as the woman I sought. I went there, and a grim and elderly woman opened the door.

"Where's John?" I inquired.

"John who?" she asked.

"John Doe," I replied; and remembering that I was a detective, added: "I am his brother."

"He isn't here," she said; at which I expressed my disappointment.

"But if you go to my sister's, she can tell you where he is living," she added a moment later.

I took the directions she gave me, and called upon the sister, and this time I asked for John and Mary, and glibly added that I was his brother.

"I knew he had a brother, but you don't look at all like him," she said critically.

"That's a fact," I agreed. "He is thin and I am stout, but I have been out West, and have changed considerably in the past few years."

"He usually calls here on his way home from work," she said. "Will you wait?"

"I don't know that I ought to," I replied. "His

mother is in poor shape and I think he ought to come home and see her. I want to talk that over with him."

She finally gave me the name of the place where he was working, and I hastened there. I was admitted to the department where they said that he was, but as I looked about at the half a dozen men there, there was not one whom I could identify as the man I sought. I stood embarrassed, for to ask that he be pointed out was to confess that I did not know him; and if he discovered this, he had but to claim another identity to have me completely baffled.

But he recognized me, and supposing that I had penetrated the disguise of his smooth-shaven face, came forward and greeted me by name.

"You used me mean, Doe," I said reproachfully, "and I have come all this way to take you back."

He was greatly disturbed, and asked permission to step from the room and speak to his employer. I consented, but accompanied him. Then he asked to be allowed to go to his rooms for necessary clothing, and I never let him out of my sight there. He had other suggestions to part company with me temporarily, but I did not rise to any of them. I did not let him out of my sight until I had surrendered him as a prisoner in my own county, and when he came into court, it was to receive a sentence of twelve months in the House of Correction.

There he labored at a trade less satisfactory than

his own, and I collected fifty cents a day for his toil, which was paid over to the partial support of his children. He had played too lightly with the chance that I offered him; but I verily believe that his story, as I related it from time to time to other probationers, kept fully a dozen recreant husbands from running away.

CHAPTER XI

In the preceding chapters I have been relating the stories of men and women saved from an impending sentence of imprisonment, and permitted through probation to return to the world of everyday affairs without the stigma of a criminal record. It may be profitable to break the narrative at this point and consider the mental attitude of the convict who is not thus rescued, but who is sent along to serve his time.

Sir Evelyn Ruggles-Brise, president of the English Prison Commission, declared in an address given at the International Prison Congress held in Washington: "Nothing in the past has so much retarded progress as the conviction deeply rooted and widespread, that the criminal is a class by himself." He went on to state that the British had been at great pains, during the past three years, by scientific and exact investigation, to disprove the popular conception of the criminal. Three thousand of the worst cases had been examined under the direction of Dr. Carl Pearson of the University College, London, and the results disclosed no evidence confirming the existence of distinct criminal types as Cesare Lombroso defined them.

My own conclusion, based on an equal number of Massachusetts cases, is that the workers of iniquity are not a race or class apart, but are merely the people who have been found out. They were but yesterday, perhaps, our neighbors on the thronging stage of life, unmarked and undistinguished from the virtuous; of the same color as the crowd. A few of them are criminals in the true sense of the word; that is to say, people who have an abnormal and unfortunate brain development that throws them inevitably into opposition to law and order. But the great majority are creatures of circumstance and environment.

Consequently, in arguing that imprisonment of itself seldom reforms the criminal,—though admittedly in the case of the professional crook confinement is necessary as a protection to society,—it is proper to inquire into the point of view of the man who is within the corrective institution. Does he admit the justice of the State's action against him? Is he convinced that the influences of the institution are working for his ultimate good? Does he retain his sense of proportions, of humor, of social relation to the world from which he has been cut off for the time being?

I have sought to obtain an answer to these questions in as impartial and accurate a manner as possible.   Eliminating the prisoner who has a special grudge against an officer or an institution, or who seeks to curry favor by feigning repentance and an appreciation of what is being done in his behalf, there still remain many men whose correspondence written from their cells, or whose observations given orally and later set down in writing at my request, permit one to form a fairly accurate estimate of their mental condition during their confinement.   Read, for example, the following impressions as set down for me by a prisoner convicted of a fairly serious offense:

"A prison is a world in itself.   Nearly every nation has its representatives here.   There are as many different tongues as the Tower of Babel; and not only variety of language, but as many different dispositions and temperaments.   A prison is a select community; but those who make it up were not selected from the head of the class.   It is hard to express what one's feelings are when dropped into such a community.   No matter what the circumstances are that bring him there, he feels like saying to himself, 'Let he who enters here leave all hope behind.'

"After the first shock is over a man begins to pull himself together and make the best he can of the situation.   He finds himself practically alone in this new world.   Nobody holds just the same ideas as himself, nor are any two of the same opinion. Yet everybody in his own mind seems to believe that he is innocent of the charge on which he was committed, and he looks upon all officers of the law as his natural enemy, and justly or unjustly he thinks that there are some men in authority who feel that position and salary depend upon finding somebody deserving of punishment every day they are on duty. In most cases prisoners feel that they are still men, who do not want to lose their identity; but it seems to me that they do not receive as much encouragement as they should.

"Men and women write and talk of us and tell us how sorry they are for our failings, and what ought to be done for us; but we feel that if we look deep down it is only on the surface with them. What men here want is something substantial in the talk of reform. Tell us what will be, not what might have been with us, and help to make that possible in a way that we can understand. Theories are of no use unless put into practice. Prisoners themselves tell what they will do when they get out, and many of them are sincere. They have felt heartaches and remorse until it seems as though the Almighty has forgotten their existence; but bye and bye something comes to lighten their load and they begin to believe that God still reigns, and hope lifts their drooping souls out of that pit of darkness.

"Some one comes here and tells us how we will be helped if we try to do right again when we get

out. We promise ourselves that we will, and we
mean it. The day comes at last when we are to go
out, and with a light heart we look at the bars on
the outer door until they look like burnished gold.
We step out into the beautiful world once more, to
breath the pure air, expecting to see the right hand
of fellowship held out in welcome. Do we find it;
not at all. We are coldly told, 'Prove that you are
worthy and we will help you.' Ah! A man who is
well does not need a physician. When we have become able to take care of ourselves we do not need
your assistance. It is when we have nowhere to
go for something to eat, and no place to sleep; when
there is nobody to give us a chance to work because
we have been in prison; then that we need the helping hand, and when it fails us, the alternative is
suicide or back to prison as a thief or a vagrant.

"The remedy for prison ills within is for those
in authority to get nearer to the inmates. Usually
those who in the highest authority are furthest
away. We are told to go to the master or the
prison commissioner when there is a complaint, but
those who really go have some special grievance,
and in many cases are agitators and kickers. The
majority are silent and scarcely thought of as individuals until the time of their discharge. Yet the
master of a prison who could get close enough to
his prisoners to have their confidence would receive it without restraint. He would then know

their needs and how to administer to them. As for those who come to talk and to pray with us for the Lord to help us to do better, we feel that such are trying to shift the responsibility of their own duty to the Almighty, asking Him to do for us what he has made them able to do themselves. We need the prayers, but we want an example of the sincerity of others when we most need help."

It is hardly necessary to add that the statement as given above has not been amplified or amended. It appears just as it was written, and one somehow draws from it the conclusion that the prison as a corrective institution has failed in its mission. This is the cry of a man who, caught in the meshes of his own sins, and unable to extricate himself, is yet not beyond the hope that some way will be found by which he may be restored to the normal life for which he has found no better substitute.

That his reference to the reception given to a discharged prisoner is true only in its broad sense does not alter the value of his argument. In Massachusetts, as will be shown in another chapter, the man whose term has expired is given both financial and moral assistance in seeking an honest livelihood, but this is temporary at best, and the business world does not modify its attitude because the State assumes that a criminal has reformed. The discharged prisoner has not been welcomed when he sought to return to a trade or a profession; and yet there is already a beginning of a changed public attitude among employers of labor. One great automobile corporation is a conspicuous example of practical philanthropy in accepting men from prisons and penitentiaries, and it has had no cause to blush for the experiment. Indeed, the greatest safeguard of the discharged prisoner is to be taken at his face value as a man who has been in wrong with the world, but who desires to "come back." The hand of fellowship is not denied to such a man, and his destiny thereafter is within his own keeping.

But let us probe the mind of another man, branded as a criminal for six years, though bearing a good New England name.

"Six years ago I knew nothing of crime or criminal life," he wrote me from his cell, on the day following a visit to him. "One winter's night in a pool room, I met two men who led me into my first crime. A month later I was arrested while trying to sell a stolen article, and found myself charged with two crimes. While awaiting trial, I thought the whole matter over alone, and finally decided to cut out the kind of life into which I had stumbled. Had any probation officer befriended me then, he could have saved me. But none came to me, and I did not know enough to send for one. I was convicted, and when the court asked me whether I had anything to say before sentence was imposed I was too nervous and excited to say anything. I got a sentence of three years in State Prison. It was my undoing. It seemed so unjust to send me there for a first offense, when I might have been committed to the Reformatory, or given a chance to reform, that I became bitter against society for punishing rather than reforming me. I came out of prison worse morally than when I went in. I came out seeking revenge, poor fool that I was to think that I alone could successfully fight organized society. That I have failed is apparent, for I have been a criminal a little over six years and have spent four and a half years of that time in prison, and am now awaiting trial again, and a life sentence, for I have contracted consumption, and can't hope to live it out. Funny, isn't it, when you think of it, that I have thrown away my life at the age of twenty-eight."

No, it is not funny; it is tragic. Some blunder of justice,—and they were more common then than in these more recent years,—made a criminal out of this young man when he was still an accidental offender, able to reform if given the chance. He had entered the game as a confused and sorry amateur, and had been graduated a prison professional. Because he believed that the law was arrayed against him, he had turned upon society in that reckless warfare of the criminal that never gives him the victory.

A few days after I received his statement the court imposed a sentence of from four to six years upon him; and it seemed to me, as I witnessed the scene, that it was one of those cases in which the clerk of the court might properly have added: "And may the Lord have mercy on your soul."

What strange beings inhabit the cell we call the body, after all! Not long ago a deputy sheriff who had been the keeper of one of our corrective institutions died, and the prisoners were permitted to come together to express their sympathy to his widow. The task of writing the letter was assigned to one of their number who had been before the courts again and again, and whose record, as one read it in the files, seemed to pledge him hopelessly to lawlessness and a disregard for the feelings of his fellow men. Yet this was the letter that he wrote; an appeal to philosophy so subtle that one is forced to wonder whether, by some strange whim of nature, his spirit was not imprisoned in a willful body quite beyond his control:

"We condole with you. We, too, have lost a most dear and valued friend; one who was ever ready and willing to offer encouragement, to listen to our individual sorrows and troubles, always ready with a helping hand in his own quiet way. But it is the will of God and nature that these mortal bodies be laid aside when the soul is about to enter into the real life.

"Let us picture this life as a preparation for living; that a man is not completely born until he is dead; and let us trust to God that a new child is born among the immortals, a new member added to their happy society. Let us be thankful for the benevolent act of God that lends us these bodies while they can afford us pleasure, or assist us in acquiring knowledge and doing good. When they become unfit for these purposes, and afford us pain, it is equally kind that a way has been provided by which we may be rid of them. Death is this way. He who plucks a tooth, parts with it freely, since the pain goes with it; and he that quits the whole body parts at once with all pains and diseases it was liable to, and therefore escapes suffering.

"Our friend and we are invited abroad on a pleasure trip that is to last forever. His chair was first ready, and he has gone before us. Since we all could not conveniently start together, let us not be grieved at this, since we are sure to follow in due time, and will know where to find him."

What irony of fate could have placed such a mind in a body so weak. Would Shakespeare, or Moore or Longfellow, meeting the writer of that letter upon the highway of life, have mistaken him for a criminal, or a poet? And yet his life has come to naught, society has found it necessary to imprison him, and the police do not hold him above suspicion while he is at large. One begins to realize, with such data available, how much salvage is yet to be rescued from the swirling stream of our prison life, when we discover the means by which we may reach the heart of the man himself.

The fourth document that I have may serve to close the chapter in lighter vein. It was written by a prisoner who signed himself Jesse, and whose dare-devil disposition, like that of his pal Tony, ultimately brought the pair to the attention of the police, who considered it advisable to put them behind lock and key for a time. Somewhere inland, and we may assume at a point considerably removed from the coast, Jesse had a sweetheart, Mary, whom he kept informed of his adventures and wanderings from time to time. In the solitude of his cell, but quite undismayed by his confinement, he wrote her the following letter, which quite concealed the identity of the place of his abode:

"Dear Mary:

"I write you a few words to let you know that Tony and I are in good health and enjoying ourselves immensely. Since coming here we have taken in all places of amusements and all historic places of interest in this part of Cambridge. Instead of taking a cottage, as has been our custom, we decided on a hotel, and find it more enjoyable and entertaining than we otherwise would if we had followed our original plan. The scenery is beautiful, and our window looks down on the prettiest garden you can imagine. The management has introduced all the improvements in the hotel and garage, and the livery is the best that I have ever come across in my career. I must also speak about the surf bathing. It is the most healthful and invigorating exercise I have ever experienced; but best of all is the total absence of intoxicating liquors here. When I was away last year on my vacation I was out of patience with the way liquor was served to the guests. I shall never forget this place as long as I live, and I shall endeavor to persuade my friends to come and enjoy themselves. I know if they come once they will make it a practice to devote some part of their years to the quiet and rest that this resort affords. Tony and I are seriously thinking of taking a lease for a few years, and if we do so, I know you will run down to visit us occasionally. We have made numerous friends here during our stay, and there are always new faces to be seen. I have been told that most of the old guests who go away for a while sooner or later come back.

"Yours with love,

"JESSE."

One may hope that Jesse was not among those who returned, attracted by the light work required, the good food, clean beds, shower baths, and ample library. A young man with that keen sense of humor should be able to find a legitimate place in the world, and not be satisfied with the role of a professional law-breaker.

But the prisoner who can treat his plight as a joke is seldom penitent, and often develops into the dangerous crook. He is not at war with society; he is seeking to beat it by cheating.

CHAPTER XII

THE FORGOTTEN MAN IN THE CELL

"Stone walls do not a prison make, nor iron bars a cage," wrote Richard Lovelace more than two hundred and fifty years ago, and added that "minds innocent and quiet take that for an hermitage." Nevertheless my own observation confirms the opinion that the innocent and the near-innocent suffer in prison much more than do those who acknowledge their guilt, and it is the duty of a probation officer to look over all the prisoners who are awaiting trial in the Superior Court, and to offer to them such assistance as the circumstances may warrant.

Very few men or women entirely innocent of the offenses with which they are charged find themselves in a cell awaiting jury trial. Police officials do not produce a prisoner to fit every crime, and oftentimes when suspicion points clearly to a person, the arrest is not made because of a lack of sufficient evidence. On the other hand, however, many arrests are made upon warrants that appear to indicate crimes of a serious nature, whereas the person involved has merely blundered into a violation of the law, less through intent than the temptation of the moment.

Naturally such a defendant, convicted in the municipal court, appeals his case to jury trial, taking advantage of a constitutional right that has saved many a man from a sentence that he appeared to merit in the heat of the first trial. I would not be understood to mean that any prisoner who refuses to accept the sentence of the lower court is better off to take his case up on appeal. In these chapters I am dealing solely with the salvage of our courts, and the application that I would make here is to those who may be saved through leniency. Time heals many wounds, and it not infrequently happens that in cases where the defendant has obtained money fraudulently, or has been convicted of assault and battery upon another, the first disposition of the party wronged is to desire that the offender be sent to prison, whereas, upon maturer reflection, he is willing to accept restitution or reparation, and so the prisoner is released and returned to the ranks of productive citizens. Or again, a defendant out on bail for several weeks, awaiting the session of the higher court, will so conduct himself in the interim that his repentance is established, and prosecuting officers deal intelligently with him, the ends of justice being served without giving him a prison record.

But to make this restitution or to live down the

disgrace of one's arrest, the man in conflict with the law must have friends to furnish his bonds when the case is appealed. If he is forced to spend the intervening weeks behind lock and key, then stone walls do a prison make, and iron bars indeed constitute a cage, in spite of the dictum of the poet.

Going my rounds in a county jail one day, just prior to the opening of the criminal session of the Superior Court, I was keeping an alert eye upon the inmates of the several cells as I passed, pausing from time to time to make the customary offer of assistance. There is a stated form in such cases. The probation officer introduces himself and invites the prisoner to write out a statement of his case from his own point of view.

"If there is anything that I can do for you after reading it, you may trust me to do so, and if there is not, I will not betray your confidence," he assures him.

Seven out of every eight so addressed accept the opportunity that this affords to discuss their troubles. Not all of them tell the truth in what they write; but a subsequent investigation of the case discloses those who may properly look to the probation officer for assistance.

I had passed by several cells, and had just made my offer anew, when a lad of seventeen met me with a broad grin, and a voice that at once suggested a famous Scotch singing comedian then touring the country.

"Where were you born?" I asked, a smile coming unconsciously to my own face.

"In Perth, Scotland," he replied, in his broad Highland voice.

"You remind me of Harry Lauder," I said. "Say something more. I enjoy hearing your voice."

"Aye, I kent Harry fine," he responded, and grinned more amply.

"You knew him well? Oh come now!"

"Aye. When he came to Perth to give his show I used to deliver handbills for him and carry his luggage to the station, and mony's the bawbees he's gied me."

"What may be your name?"

"They caa' me Bobbie," he answered.

"You've not been over long, though."

"We cam oot a matter of ten months since."

"And what got you into trouble?"

"I stole a pair of rubber boots on the Fourth of July. They sent me up, but I've appealed."

The Scotch jaw set like a trap, and the grin died out of his face. I consulted my list. He had been given an interdeterminate sentence that might hold him for five years, and the least he could hope for if it was confirmed was a minimum of fifteen months in addition to his present confinement. Stealing rubber boots in July! What sort of a mad prank was this; and the lad already branded a criminal, and tucked away here without friends. I determined to sift his case thoroughly.

"Harry Lauder has given me more than one hour's good fun, and for his sake I am going to help the chap who put out his handbills," I told him. "Where are your people living?"

He told me; and later in the day I found them, his parents and six or seven brothers and sisters. The father was a baker, who had come to the States from Scotland to better his condition. Very naturally, they were living in a poor tenement quarter of the city, where the children of immigrants are always put under peculiar temptations by their new environment.

The mother talked to me about Bobbie. He was a good son, but a bit "e-responsible," she declared sorrowfully. When a small child he had fallen over a bannister, landing upon his head, and he had been a little "light" at times since then, though all right in the main.

I recalled "the saftest o' them a'" in Harry Lauder's song, and leaving the meagre home continued my investigations as to the circumstances of the crime. On the night of the Fourth, I learned, —the glorious anniversary of American Independence, when even native-born citizens have been

known to do rash and technically unlawful deeds,—
Bobbie and two other boys younger than himself
had broken into a freight car standing on a siding,
and a pair of rubber boots had been stolen.   These
had been traced to the cellar of Bobbie's home; and
the arrest of the oldest of the trio had followed,
and he had been sentenced to the Reformatory.   It
is a wonder that the lad knew enough to appeal, for
in his own country such sentence would have been
final, and therefore accepted without question.

I had no hesitation in asking the judge to place
the boy on probation when his case came up for
disposal, but I was not prepared to return him to
his own home.   If I assumed the responsibility for
his freedom, I also took upon myself the burden of
the reformation that the State was otherwise willing
to undertake in its own way.   Bobbie's parents obviously had their hands full until they were better
established.   Their economic struggle to maintain
themselves in a country where the cost of living
was much greater than in Scotland left them no
time to reorganize the tenement quarter in which
they found themselves, or to select fit companions
for their children.   Moreover, the lad must not lose
sight of the fact that he had done an unlawful act.

Now I happened to know a big-hearted Irish con-
tractor, for whom the name of Moran will serve in
this narrative, who had no child of his own, and
who had said to me upon one occasion: "When

the right boy comes along, send him over.   I'll learn him a trade, and perhaps I'll do better by him." There are many Morans in my work, both men and women, born under many flags, rich and poor, who understand the unfortunates of the world, and who, time after time, have helped me start them anew. Much of the success of this reform work is due to them, and not to myself.

So I called Mr. Moran on the telephone, and I said to him: "Have you ever heard Harry Lauder sing?"

"Sure I have, and not done laughing yet," he replied.

"I've got a second edition of him," I explained. "If your offer for a lad is still open, I want you to have a talk with him."

"Hang on to him," shouted Moran.   "I'll come right over."

"He will be here all right," I assured him. "They've got him locked up in a cell until I get him out on probation."

Mr. Moran came right over, though he was some considerable distance away.   When the Irish and the Scotch agree on anything, it is a rare sight, and friendships come of it that are not to be broken. Moran solemnly cross-questioned Bobbie as to what he knew about horses, and to his delight the lad responded in the Perth dialect.   When I explained the situation to the judge, he accepted a plea from

the young man and released him on his good behavior. Bobbie went from the court room with his
new found friend, and for many months thereafter
worked for him, and lived in his own house as a
member of the family.

And that period permitted Bobbie's family to ad-
just itself to its new problems. At the end of a
year the father was earning $25 a week and had
moved to a better house in another city. He now
wanted the son home with him; and Moran bade
him a reluctant good-by, having become genuinely
fond of him.

Because I had the feeling that I might have passed
this case over unnoticed in the rush of a particularly
busy month, had not the young man reminded me
of Harry Lauder, I wrote a letter to the Scotch
comedian, giving him credit for having indirectly
saved the boy who had once served him. Lauder
wrote me characteristically in reply from Notting-
ham, England, as follows: "I was pleased to read
that I had come in time to save a laddie. I trust
he will learn to show his gratitude to his timely
friends—and when I again visit Boston come and
see me and have a shake o' the hand."

Bobbie has not disappointed us. It was his first,
and probably his last offense; yet we might have
branded him a criminal, and then turned him loose
in the new land of liberty with false notions of its
laws and customs. Had we done so, neither he nor

his family nor the State itself would have benefited by the process; a fact so obvious that it is unnecessary to argue it further.

Upon another occasion I had entered the corridor of a prison where two men were awaiting trial for murder, one of them for a crime that had shocked the entire country. They occupied separate cells, with an intervening one between, and in this I discovered a man who had been unable to obtain bail, and who was awaiting trial on a charge of embezzlement. His appearance suggested a man above the usual grade of prison inmates, and his first words served to confirm the impression.

"Christ hung between two thieves, and I am here between two murderers," he said. "The thought of that is my only compensation."

I drew him into a conversation, and very soon discovered that he was deeply religious, and had been the superintendent of a Sunday school. The world is prone to be harsh in its judgment of the church official who goes astray, holding, quite properly, perhaps, that his vows should have kept him strong in temptation, but I felt an immediate interest in this man's case, and went out from the prison to see what could be done for him.

The year had been one of great industrial depression, which had brought many men from a comfortable income to near-poverty. John Raymond was an insurance agent, with a good territory and doing an excellent business up to that time; but insurance as a purchasable commodity is something that the public can do without when trade is poor or work slack. His income began to decrease until it no longer sufficed to support his family, and he began to get into debt. After a time his creditors dunned him for payment.

Every insurance man knows that there are periods in his soliciting that yield almost no return; but they often pass as quickly as they come on. One-half of the United States is always predicting a boom just ahead, and at this time optimistic Americans who were whistling to keep up their courage were saying that very soon there would be a decided turn for the better. John Raymond, hard pressed for money, and seeking only temporary relief, had a check for $425 pass through his hands in settlement for a death claim of one of his clients. The widow to whom it was payable was not in immediate want, and he induced her to make the paper over to him, promising to give her his own check at the end of two months.

With this sum he paid his bills and breathed easier for a time. But the business of the country did not improve. It seemed as though nobody would ever care to buy insurance policies again; and at the end of two months he had not a cent to his credit in the bank. He made excuses to the widow, and she gave him an extension of time.

He faced a serious situation now, realizing that something must be done at once to meet a crisis that was merely postponed. The insurance business was dead,—for the time being, at any rate,—and he must seek employment at some other occupation. "I was quite willing to do this," he told me later, "but not in the place where I was known as an insurance agent."

He went to a city in the western part of the state, and obtained employment in a store. His friends during that period included two clergymen, who later assured me that every incident of his life there indicated that he was seeking to support his family and obtain money to pay back the sum that he owed. Yet what followed was almost inevitable. The widow became alarmed at his absence and his failure to keep his word to her, and made a complaint to the police. They found the circumstances of his departure suspicious, traced him to the city where he had gone, brought him back under arrest, and here he was, after a preliminary hearing, held in a thousand dollars awaiting trial. He had been unable to raise the bail, and had been an occupant of this cell for two months, his wife and children supported in the meantime by the Lodge of Odd Fellows to which he belonged.

"I have been unfaithful to a trust, but I have not committed a crime," he protested; yet I knew well enough that no jury would make this distinction, but that he would be found guilty on the facts as he himself was willing to admit them.

It seemed to me that here was an opportunity to save a man by probation if only I could satisfy the claim against him. He was forty-four years of age, and his whole life up to that time had been exemplary. During his years of prosperity he had lived well, but had given liberally to charity, and once a year had sent a check to the Salvation Army in Boston to aid those who were unfortunate. He had been punished already until his cup was running over, and he asked only that he be given a chance to return to the support of his family, to whom he was devoted.

I put it up to the Odd Fellows, and although they had been maintaining his family all this time, they raised $50 for me. But it was all that they were able to do, and the best settlement that I could obtain from the widow was a promise to accept $300. Unless I could obtain $250 at once, there was no way in which the trial of the case could be averted.

To many of you who read, this raising of a few hundred dollars for a man in prison may seem a simple matter. I assure you that it is quite otherwise. There were any number of people who wished me success in my effort to obtain the release of John Raymond, but when it came to talking real money, they felt that they must look more thoroughly into the matter. They had been counted as friends of this man in his prosperity; but the circumstances were different now—he had been arrested, and they felt that subscribing money to aid him was like giving it to charity. They didn't feel sure that he would be able to pay them back, handicapped as he would be by the publicity of his misfortune.

But I found a man at last, though he was a complete stranger to me at the time. I had come to the afternoon of the last day in the year, and the case might be called at any moment now. I hurried over to State Street in Boston, the financial district of the city, because somebody had told me that Frank A. Day, of the banking firm of R. L. Day & Co., was a man of large heart and wide charity.

I sent in my card, and was ushered into his private office. He was a most courteous man to meet, but his, "Well, what can I do for you?" as he glanced at my card again was nothing more than a polite request to state my errand. I told him the story of John Raymond, briefly but as earnestly as I knew how, and I could see by the line of inquiry on his brow that he was trying to connect it with himself to discover just why he should be called upon for assistance.

"My only excuse in coming here is that he is a citizen of your city, and a man worth saving from prison," I said.

"But would you do this thing yourself?" he asked

shrewdly. Many an eloquent charity beggar is careful that his own salary does not go the way of his business, and Mr. Day knew this.

"I can't afford to," I said quite frankly. "But I know that you give to worthy charity, and here is an unusual opportunity to accomplish definite good. You stand between this man and prison, and it is in your power to set him free."

"Yes, but—"

"And your reward will come in the satisfaction that you will feel tomorrow when you realize that you have given this man back to his family as a New Year's gift."

He touched a bell on his desk and said to the clerk who responded: "Bring me $250 in bills, charged to my personal account." When it came he handed me the money. That was all.

No, that was not all. In the first place, the sum released Raymond and sent him to his waiting home, and within a week I had secured a place for him with another insurance company, and that was the beginning of better days for him. He not only lived down his disgrace, but he has since been devoting his spare time to warning other men against the temptations of the business world. I have heard him hold an audience spellbound in a city church, and he speaks from knowledge and suffering.

But the more wonderful part of the experience

for me was the fact that Mr. Day's assistance did not end with Raymond. He became so interested in my work that he asked to be permitted to share in other similar cases; and he began to visit the homes of the poor with me, and ere long had become known as "the assistant probation officer." We became close friends in the work, and he would often slip away from his large business interests to meet me for a week-end and talk over the misfortunes of the young fellows who had been plucked out of the maelstrom through his generosity.

And in the midst of this good work Death reached out a finger of malignant malady and beckoned to him. He was not frightened, because he was ready; and we watched him being drawn slowly from us, powerless to save him. In those last days I had two messages from him, which should be laid as a wreath upon his memory.

In the first he asked me to take his two sons out into the slums, "to see how the poor live, that they may not grow up in selfishness." And just before his death he said: "Caution men in middle life to read good books, for the time may come to them, as it has to me, when living is irksome unless they have something on which to depend for comfort."

God rest him. He was a man who went from life with clean hands, and a heart undefiled.

So in neither of the cases that I have cited in this chapter do I claim any credit for myself. Here was salvage rescued by other men whose elbows had touched mine in the busy press of life.   How many times since then have I found similar help from private sources available.

CHAPTER XIII

THE EXCESSIVE SENTENCE THAT DOES NOT REFORM

A Southern editor once told me, in the expressive language of a semi-tropical Baptist, that he would be willing to go to hell for one day in order that he might ask the Devil why he fell so low. "Continued sin is illogical," he argued. "Even a fiend incarnate would satiate himself with it eventually."

Continued sin is illogical, and a genuine biography of the Devil, if written, would prove of peculiar psychological interest. Our orthodox point of view can explain it only upon the assumption that Satan is a generator of evil, otherwise he could not remain permanently at the bottom of the pit.

"And yet the Bible tells us that he was originally an angel, who fell from high estate," replied the Southerner when I advanced this argument. "I don't believe that an angel or a man who starts right can go to the bottom of the mire and be completely satisfied with his career."

Concerning the process of mental degeneration of the Prince of Darkness I have no data; but I do know the story of James Bond, "the worst man who ever occupied a cell in the Massachusetts Prison." That was the characterization of him by prison officials, and I have no reason to dispute it. Partly because of the point raised by the Southern editor, and more particularly because I desired to study the antecedents of a case quite beyond the pale of parole or probation, I had asked for the name of a prisoner who could be considered, for devilish brutality, or criminal ingenuity, or some similar qualification, so far removed from redemption that there could be no question of the right of the State to confine him.

And they gave me the name of James Bond, which, by one of those inexplicable ironies of fate, was not that of a stranger. In the old days when I was in charge of a switch tower on a New England railroad, he was employed by the same corporation as a brakeman, and many a time had I set the switches for his train, little anticipating that the time would come that should see us both in a new and strange relation.

Somebody has said that there lies in the heart of all of us the seeds of great good or great evil, and that whichever grows to flower first will choke out the other. James Bond had given no sign of evil, so far as I know, until a day when he met with an accident in the course of his work upon the railroad, and disputed the extent of his injuries. He was then a man under twenty-five, and married to a good woman.

Yet his was a spirit born for the contest of wits,

of which there was early and unmistakable evidence. As a boy of ten he caused consternation one day by rushing into the schoolroom with the cry that he had seen a man killed on the railroad outside. He gave every detail of the accident, and the session of the school was temporarily suspended while the teacher hastened to spread the alarm. Yet no body was found, for the tale was a pure fabrication. The boy, yearning for excitement, had created it out of his own imagination.

In time he grew to manhood and found employment upon this very railroad. He was steady, industrious, apparently normal up to the day when he was carried to a hospital. While he was confined there the relief society to which he belonged paid him a benefit of $5 a week, but the railroad surgeon who examined him reported that his injury was not serious, and that he would be around all right in a short time.

But James Bond refused to recover as the physician had promised. He declared that his lower limbs had become paralyzed, and that he was crippled for life. The claim agent of the railroad scoffed at the idea; but Bond engaged able counsel, and entered suit to recover damages. The case attracted wide attention, and brought forth an array of experts. The defendant corporation alleged that the plaintiff was feigning injury, and had their physicians probe his limbs with sharp needles. Bond

met this test without flinching.   He remained paralyzed in court until the jury returned him a verdict
of $8000.   Three months later he had recovered.

Of course occupation upon the railroad was
closed to him, but he was amply supplied with
money, and opened a lodging house.   Sentiment
was not entirely friendly to him, and he began to
grow careless as to his companions.   One of them
was a young woman whom he had known in his
unmarried days, and whose company he now began
to frequent.   They were out late together one night
when the girl's father stepped in and charged the
man with improper intimacy.   He demanded $100
indemnity for his outraged parental feelings.

Bond laughed at him, and retorted that the girl
was no better than she ought to be, and knew quite
well what she was doing.   The father swore out
a warrant, and the officer who sought to serve it
found that his man had quietly slipped out of the
state.   A detective was put upon the case, with
orders to find Bond and bring him back.   The
notoriety of the $8000 verdict had not yet subsided,
and here was additional proof that James Bond was
as bad a man as had been alleged.

He was brought back, and the girl took the stand
against him.   Whatever her real status may have
been, the fact remains that standing between her
father upon the one hand and the defendant upon
the other, she testified in support of the story that

she had told the former. Bond was found guilty and sentenced to prison for a term of fifteen years.

Now to gain the proper understanding of his mental attitude from this moment, we must concede that he considered himself unjustly punished. He had committed a crime, because the girl was below the age of consent, and by no line of reasoning should he have been exempt from punishment. But he believed that the sentence over-reached the crime, and from that moment he was in rebellion against the State. He saw red as soon as the fateful words were uttered, dashing his head against the dock in a fury of madness that brought the court officers hurrying to overpower him. In prison he became known almost immediately as an incorrigible, and was early marked for close observation.

In spite of this fact he devised a plan of escape that in boldness exceeded anything in the long history of the institution. In one corner of the yard, within the shadow of the great granite wall, was an opening into a sewer where slops and dirty water were thrown by the "trusties" of the prison. This sewer was kept flushed by the incoming tide from the river, a tide-water stream into which the sewer opened, several hundred rods away. Twice every twenty-four hours the water backed up until it closed the bottom of the opening in the prison yard.

Yet down into this sewer went Bond and several other long-term prisoners, though no man among them knew whether the pipe underground gave sufficient opening to permit the foul journey in the darkness to the river. The feat of Jean Valjean in "Les Miserables" was less dangerous than these desperate men performed.

When the absence of the prisoners was noted, and their avenue of escape discovered, one man was found lodged in the sewer, where he would have met his death had he not been rescued. The others had escaped, and a hundred police began to scour the country for them. Bond was found in the woods of Belmont, several miles away, on the following day, carrying an exhausted fellow convict upon his back. Had he abandoned the man he might have escaped; but he remained with him.

A prisoner who runs away and is brought back receives an additional sentence and forfeits the right to have his original term shortened for good behavior. But Bond plotted anew with deep cunning. On a day when a score of prisoners were assembled in the guard room he raised his hand as a signal, and each convict leaped upon the guard nearest to him. A desperate fight followed, for in some mysterious manner the prisoners had obtained arms. Blood was shed, but the outbreak was quelled, and nobody escaped.

For this feat Bond had seven years and twenty-three days added to his sentence, and was placed in permanent close confinement. For eleven years thereafter he lived apart from the other prisoners, an inmate of his narrow cell, seeing no man other than the occasional prison official who passed down the corridor.

When a man is placed in this solitary confinement there is no escape for him except through death or insanity. Men not infrequently go mad under such circumstances, and when they become broken mentally they are removed to an asylum for the criminally insane. Bond appeared to go insane, and that he had lost his reason was the general opinion of those who were permitted to see him. But the deputy warden, a capable, just man, was not deceived. He would not permit the inmate of the cell to be removed.

The degradation to which this man descended during the two years that followed is almost beyond belief, and quite beyond discussion. For twenty-four months he simulated madness, crawling about upon his hands and knees, stripping all his clothing from his body, refusing to speak, matching his wits against the ironical, unconvinced warden.

"Come out of it," demanded the latter at length, disgusted with the long pretense. "You will never get better treatment until you do."

Bond became a normal man again. His plan to escape by way of the asylum had failed.

Then, one day, there came a councillor of the state to visit the prison.   By virtue of his pardoning power as a member of the Governor's Council he had the right to speak to the prisoners, and he asked to be taken to the cell of this man in solitary.

The interview that took place between them had a marvelous effect upon James Bond.   He gave his word that if restored to the privilege of working with the other prisoners, and of walking in the yard, he would plot no more against the prison authorities; and in proof of his intention he spoke to the warden for the first time in eight years.   It had taken fifteen years to break the stubborn spirit of this man who believed himself to have been wronged, and one might naturally inquire now as to the mental condition in which this long struggle had left him.   It is this phase of the case that warrants my telling the story in such detail.

I sought to do something for him as soon as he came out of solitary confinement, realizing that if he was one day to obtain his release, something must be done to fit him for the world from which he had been so long cut off.   After the years of his silence and degradation, it offered a rare problem to discover what manner of man still survived within the body.   I retain among my papers the letter that he wrote me during this period.

"I have not forgotten your kindness to me," he said.   "You know we can not write from here when we want to, and when we do it is quite an event, I assure you. I have always felt just as happy and thankful when contemplating what you tried to do for me as if you had accomplished everything. And my poor Greely is dead. Well, words cannot express my feelings for him."

He went on to speak of several others whom he had known in the days of his freedom, and concerning whose death he had only now learned: "And Conners is dead; such a tough and rugged little fellow. The last Sunday that I was free we spent together. As I stood in the hospital the other day and listened to the nurse recount the number of men who had died while I was in solitary, I could not help but thank God for His love and care of me. I have always felt an influence as one loved and cared for, and I attribute it to the prayers I know loving hearts are daily sending to God for me."

I paused in the reading of the letter to readjust myself to these words. I had finished the book of a noted European criminologist only a day or two before, and if the theories advanced by him were sound, such a man as this was a criminal from birth, pre-natally marked for crime, and therefore with almost no hope of redemption. I had also to consider the months of feigned insanity, when he had sunk so low that even the hardened prison guards had shuddered at the thought of him. There should be no memory of God surviving in the mind of such a man! There could be but scant hope of salvation through the power of prayer for one so deep in sin! And yet his written words confessed it. In the hours of his bitterest rebellion he had been conscious of some influence still trying to save him.

I resumed the reading of the letter, which now gave vivid glimpses of his prison life: "Fourteen years ago there came to the prison one Sunday a young slip of a girl to sing for us, and she has continued to come all the time since. But being in solitary, I had not seen her for twelve years. About a month ago, the chaplain told us, her husband, an engineer on the New Haven road, died. To-day when I went to the chapel I saw a woman in widow's weeds, sitting by the chaplain's side; and soon I recognized the slip of a girl, now grown to be a beautiful woman. In those twelve years she had suffered, too. She soon rose and sang for us a song that contained the words, 'There are shadows in the valley, but there is sunshine on the hill.' When the prisoners thought of her devotion to us, and when she revealed the beauty of her character through this song, the strongest hearts burst into tears. There are a number of these Christian people who come here to lighten our burden; but not a tenth as many as ought to. They can never understand the comfort and solace that they bring to us in this Egypt."

Egypt, the land of bondage! I thought to myself that probably very few who faced that silent, sullen congregation within the prison walls honestly believed that either comfort or solace was given by the service; and yet here was the testimony of the worst man in the institution, who was just groping his way back toward the light.

Once more I turned to the letter. "My prison life has been greatly alleviated," it continued. "A lad I used to 'brake' with on the railroad has become a wealthy business man in Boston, and he has been working for me ever since he discovered my plight. He has ordered me every comfort that is allowed, and has urged me to buy at his expense all the books I want. But, at present, the chaplain has placed his private library at my disposal, and I can take from it all the books I wish and keep them as long as I want. This would be no small treat anywhere. So you see that God is still good to me in more ways than one. And did I tell you how I got out of solitary? It was through a working girl, now married to a member of the Governor's Council, to whom I once did a kindness."

Professor Hugo Munsterberg has observed that our subconscious mind is the sum total of all our registered experiences and impressions. Is not life, in part at least, the sum total of the friends and enemies that we make? In this letter was the evidence that the friends of James Bond, made in his better days, were finally bringing about his regeneration; and perhaps if we could go back into his earliest years we might find there the elements that also impelled him to crime.   One often notes in the lives of what we term the criminal class such influences working at cross purposes.   The man within the body,—"the spirit at the helm," as one writer has termed it,—is sometimes so weak that the baser influences prompt his actions for so long a time that there seems to be no hope for him.   Then, at the eleventh hour, comes a realization of the useless waste of it all, and the baneful influences in his life begin to lose their power.

It was so with this man.   He began to store his mind with clean things from the books placed at his disposal, and to reëstablish his relations with the world outside the granite walls.   Prison guards ceased to think of him as a bad man; and because of his change of heart, his old friends took courage to work for his pardon, that he might begin life anew.

One day in April I received the following letter from him, though the news that it contained did not come as a surprise: "You will be happy to learn that I am once more among the free.   And I would be happy could I go back to the city where I once lived, and see my old and dear friends, but circumstances will not permit.   For the kind words you have always said of me, which have come to me year after year in prison, you can little judge of the comfort and strength that they brought.   It will be the endeavor of my life now to prove that I am a far better man than even my friends believe possible. You advise me in your letter to so circumscribe my actions when I get out of prison as to retain the good opinion of everybody.   You need have no fear of me.   I will see that my friends never blush for any unmanly act of mine."

That was several years ago, and he has resided since then in another state, seeking to live down a notoriety that made it virtually impossible to return to the scenes once familiar to him.   He is doing well; inconspicuous as one of the great multitude of normal, law-respecting citizens.

"Which proves my contention," observed the Southern editor when I cited the facts as I have given them here.   "Continued sin is illogical."

"But a man in prison who considers himself overpunished is never logical," I pointed out.

"Which merely means that it takes him longer to find it out," he replied.   "This man sacrificed the best years of his life because he could not see that sin did not pay."

"Was it the original sin, or the rebellion against punishment that made him a desperate prisoner?" I asked, turning a question I could not answer back to him.

"One blossomed into the other," he parried

neatly. "He had set himself out to get things in life outside the law, and God pulled him up short."

"God, or the law?"

"The law pulled him up," he corrected, and added: "But I don't believe it reformed him."

"What did reform him?"

"What made the prodigal son arise from the husks that the swine were eating, and decide to return to his father?"

We pursued this discussion at some length, each arriving at his own conclusion, as theorists will.

But my own experience has taught me that in working among men and women who have gone astray, one can not follow a given rule. Human beings are as different as their finger prints, which look very similar to the uninitiated, but which yield surprising variations and distinctions when accurately recorded. Therefore we cannot, from what data we are likely to have on hand in most cases, invariably classify criminals or prescribe remedies that will fit them exactly. There is always the individual variation to be taken into account.

I am not even prepared to say that this man, had he been given a light sentence or probation for the offence that brought him before the bar of justice, might have been rescued years before, and so averted a long term of suffering inflicted upon himself and his family. Possibly fate ordained that this struggle was necessary before he was freed from himself; though why, after all, should fate take so much trouble with any of us! But I do stand behind the conclusion that no man falls so low that he cannot come up again through the power that is within himself. Therefore this chapter is written for men and women who are in desperate rebellion, who have sounded the depths of hell in their war against restraining order, and who believe that the hands of all mankind are turned against them. No one of you can go so low but that he will find the mark in the bottom of the pit made there by James Bond.

And even in such a hell, the prayers of good women reached this man, and healed his torment!

CHAPTER XIV

In the early years of my service as an officer of the court, I could not have anticipated, by any exercise of the imagination, that the time would come when my list of probationers would include those who had taken human life. Yet several men have been given over to my custody who have shed human blood.

Strictly speaking, such men are not placed on probation, but are released with the probation officer as their surety for good behavior; nor should one speak of them, except in the broad sense, as murderers. They have killed one who had the right to his life, but the act had not been premeditated, and may have been committed in fear or under some other emotion aroused by unforeseen circumstances. Yet the trial of such cases is oftentimes most difficult, because it is not always possible to uncover all the incidents that led up to the deed. The public mind has long been trained to believe that any person who kills should receive the death penalty or a long term of imprisonment, the theory being that only such punishment will prevent other men from becoming murderers.

Dismissing from our consideration the premeditated murder, and the one committed in the heat of passion from a latent impulse to kill, both of which strip the murderer of all his rights other than that of a fair trial, there remains another class with which the courts have begun to deal from an enlightened point of view. Let me offer two typical cases under this head, in which the reader may ask himself whether severe punishment would accomplish anything for society if administered.

My first case of manslaughter was that of an Armenian, and I did not enter into it until the judge before whom the defendant had pleaded guilty had imposed a sentence of one year in the House of Correction. Of course there were mitigating circumstances to merit so light a sentence. As briefly stated by the prosecuting attorney when the prisoner was called before the bar for judgment, the Armenian, who was thirty-two years of age, had borne an excellent reputation so far as known since coming to this country. He had struck a fellow farm hand under some provocation, and the single blow had caused death. The Armenian was represented by counsel of his own nationality, who appeared to be satisfied with the minimum sentence imposed.

There was no real warrant for my intrusion in a

case where my services had not been required by
the Court, but I am impelled to cite the facts just
as they occurred, because they shed an illuminating
light upon the character of our Massachusetts
judges, which it is not possible for the private citizen to obtain.   I had no reason to believe that this
particular judge would favorably consider probation for so serious an offense, and I realized that
the defendant's counsel was the one to offer any unusual circumstance that favored him; yet I made
bold to enter the private room of the justice during
a recess of the Court, to tell him that I believed that
a further investigation of the case would bring new
evidence to light.   I had discovered that the real
instigator of the crime was a boy who had broken
his parole, and this fact had not been stated to the
Court.

An odd incident favored me, for as I opened the
door I discovered the judge, a broomstick in hand,
explaining to the sheriff of the county the manner
in which the blow was delivered.   Whereupon I
told him what my own theory of the case was, and
asked that it might be reopened for further inquiry.
It was late in the afternoon; there was other business awaiting the attention of the Court; and the
lawyer for the defense had now left the Court
House.   Yet the judge promptly recalled the case
when his Court reconvened, revoked the sentence
that he had imposed, and remanded the prisoner for

one day. The case was then in my hands for investigation, and I lost no time in beginning my inquiry. And these were the facts as I found them:

The Armenian had come to this country as a refugee from a Turkish massacre a few years before, penniless, and bearing the scars from freshly healed bayonet wounds. The United States has afforded a refuge to thousands of such men, who, having come under the influence of the American mission schools in Turkey, have turned their anguished eyes to these shores in their hour of peril, expecting here protection and a friendly understanding. But this man found, as had the others, a great nation quite too busy to inquire into the welfare of any single immigrant. His story and the few dollars that he was able to show gained him an admission at the Port of New York, but he was left to his own devices thereafter, and finally found employment on the farm of an Irish-American in Massachusetts. The family was poor, and the hired help, this man and two boys under eighteen, occupied a common room in the attic of the house, the Armenian sleeping upon a couch and the boys occupying a bed.

The help were well treated, but the hours were long and the work hard. The Armenian soon became the handy man upon the farm, while the boys drove a milk wagon. All three were accustomed to retire before nine o'clock at night, in order to be up before daybreak in the morning. This routine had gone on for many months, when a younger brother of one of the boys appeared at the farm one day, and asked to be put up for the night. He was permitted to sleep in the bed with the other two, and on the morrow he did not go away as expected, but made himself useful about the place, so that the good-natured Irishman fed him and permitted him to stay.

Now this boy was on probation and had run away, and his purpose in remaining at the farm was to keep out of reach of the officer who might be looking for him. This fact is important as precipitating the tragedy that followed.

There is no evidence that the Armenian was ever at odds with his room-mates until this lad, with surplus deviltry in his system, arrived at the farm. The boys were steady at their work and regular in their hour of retiring at night. But one evening, when the older boy and the Armenian turned in, the brothers were missing, and had not returned when the other occupants of the room fell asleep.

Indeed, the whole household was asleep when the younger boys came in, primed for mischief. The probationer proposed that they play a trick on the Armenian, and suggested that they get some pepper and place it on his nose, so that he would breathe it into his nostrils. One may pass over the utter and unwarranted folly of this act, indefensible from any point of view, and to be explained only by the rashness of youth, to note its dire consequences. The pepper-box was carried upstairs, the boys undressed, and just before they slipped into bed they shook the irritant in the face of the sleeping man.

He began to sneeze, and awakening, involuntarily rubbed his hands over his face. The pepper was carried to the eyes; and smarting with pain, and still unaware of what had happened, he sprang from the couch, half blinded, and ran from the room in search of water, half suppressed laughter following him from the bed. But when he returned, still in great pain, and muttering in rage, the boys had become frightened, and had crawled under the bed.

The older boy, exhausted by the day's hard toil, still slept soundly. The moonlight, dimly lighting the room, might have disclosed this fact to one whose vision was unimpaired.

Back to the chamber came the Armenian, armed with a broomstick. He had only a few elemental facts at his command. He had retired with one other person in the room, and an unnatural trick had been played upon him while he slept, bringing laughter from the other bed. Once before in his life he had been the victim of an unprovoked attack, when his fellow Armenians had been done to death. It is impossible to tell just what may have been the emotions that prompted him to strike one blow at the figure in the bed, apparently feigning sleep.

The blow fell upon the temple of the sleeping man. With a terrible cry he sprang up, sat for a moment on the edge of the bed moaning with pain and bleeding inwardly, and then fell back dead. A sordid story this; yet who was the one to blame for the crime? Not the Armenian, but the young boy who had broken his parole, and had forced himself upon these three regular occupants of the attic bedroom. The death was really upon his head, even if the law did not lay its hand upon him.

I told this story to the Court, with no more dramatic force than these facts as I have related them here seemed to warrant. He was a judge of the old school, trained in the teaching of an eye for an eye and a tooth for a tooth; but he was a wise man, whose justice had always been tempered with mercy. He ordered the release of the Armenian on his good behavior, and I went surety for him.

When the grateful man left the court room he hastened to Boston to inform his lawyer of the turn in the tide of his affairs; and the latter was so certain that he had escaped from prison that he all but gave him up to the police again. I obtained work for him, and the great industrial world soon swallowed him up among its countless workers. He has given no further trouble to the Commonwealth. Yet the fact remains that he killed a man. What would a year in confinement have done for him? The deed, not contemplated in its fatal termination, was done under great provocation, and, in a measure, in self-defense. Our justice has probably done more for him than punishment would have accomplished.

So much for the first case. Passing over several in the intervening years, I come to one that has only recently occupied my attention, and that offers quite unusual opportunity for intimate study and analysis of the motives involved.

I found in a cell one day a man fifty-nine years old, a modern Cain, under indictment for the killing of his brother, two years his junior. Was it not Cicero who cleared a prisoner from the charge of parricide by arguing that he could not have committed such an unnatural crime and remained unmoved by it? Here was a case of fratricide that was an exception to such an argument. The prisoner stood ready to plead guilty to the fact of having killed his brother, but he did not consider that he had committed a crime. He said that he had killed him as the climax to a quarrel, but that he had acted in self-defense. While confined in prison awaiting the sitting of the Court he ate well, slept soundly, and was entirely indifferent as to what became of him.

My preliminary investigation of the case yielded only the surface facts. The two brothers were unmarried,—"old baches," as the neighbors called them—and had kept house in the country. There

was a third brother who had worked his way
through college and who was successful now in his
profession in a neighboring city; but these two had
always lived at home, their education limited, their
daily experience restricted to humble things.

There was a disposition on the part of the district
attorney to deal leniently in the case, and sentiment
in the village rather favored the brother under arrest.   It was the opinion that he had been "nagged"
by the dead man, who had been in the wrong at the
beginning of the quarrel.   Jim Benson himself was
not a bad man, said his neighbors, because he was
one of the town constables.

My next step was to sound the state of the prisoner's mind.   A probation officer under such circumstances is the eyes and ears of the Court.   He
is not a detective, seeking to discover new evidence
that may aid the prosecution, but rather is an unofficial aid to the judge, who can not come into this
personal relation with a defendant about to be tried.
In introducing myself to Benson I assured him that
I had come to be of service to him, and in other
words I sought to gain his confidence.   But I went
away without having accomplished anything at all.
He would not talk.   He viewed me as an unknown
factor in his affairs, to be regarded with suspicion.

Again I went to his cell and told him something
of the nature of my work.   He unbent a little and
related the bare facts of the tragedy.   They were

recited without emotion. It was much as though the dead brother was within hearing, and he wanted him to realize that the outcome of the dispute was not his, Jim's, fault.

I now asked him to write out the facts in the case for me, since pent-up feelings will sometimes find an outlet through the pen. A man past middle life is schooled to suppress his real emotions, but in the solitude of a written confession may disclose the motives that prompted his actions. Jim Benson's confession yielded no clue beyond the fact that he had been, in his own opinion, only a passive agent to the homicide. He did not argue in his own behalf. He offered no mitigating circumstance as a justification for imposing the minimum sentence. If the State desired to confine him for the remainder of his life, he would accept the sentence as something quite beyond his control.

"There is one chance that the Court may release you and permit you to return home," I said.

Offer this hope of release to any normal man who has been in prison for many weeks awaiting trial, and he will grasp at it as a drowning man reaches for a life belt thrown to him. But it did not move Jim Benson at all. He did not seem to care one way or the other, and it became apparent to those of us who studied his case that continued imprisonment would not constitute punishment in any real sense. Neither time nor space appeared to exist for the man. I question whether he would have left his cell voluntarily had the door been open and escape suggested to him.

The judge did release him. Benson was called to the bar to plead guilty to the complaint, and he was then placed in my charge to keep the peace. This fact meant not only his own freedom, but the lifting of a burden from the heart of the successful brother, who had grieved for the dead and pleaded for the probation of the living. Here was a moment capable of arousing a great emotion, and I looked for some outburst of belated feeling; but it did not come. Jim Benson left the court-room as though walking from his kitchen to the woodshed, and when I sat down to talk with him in another part of the building, he called me by my first name, as he had overheard my associates do.

His brother took him back to the old home, but not before I had impressed upon his mind the importance of the letters that he would now be required to write to me regularly as one of the terms of his probation. I warned him that he was not yet legally free, but had been released upon his good behavior, and that I was responsible for him, and must be kept informed of his actions from week to week.

Naturally I awaited with more than ordinary interest the receipt of that first letter, which was to disclose to me something of his state of mind when he found himself back in the home where he and the dead brother had so long shared their common life. Would not the past surge over him, breaking down his reserve of indifference? Would not the memories of his father and mother come back to him, pointing an accusing finger at the blood that had been shed! Cicero would have so argued centuries ago; and philosophers tell us that mankind does not change within.

"How do you do; pretty well?" Jim Benson wrote me in his first letter. "That is good. I am the same, pegging away as usual. It is cold down here. How is it up there? Cold, you bet. Well, it will soon be spring, and the birds will be here. I like to hear them sing, don't you? Especially the brown thrush. Did you ever hear one sing? He will sing for an our at a time. I know. I was working on a road that goes to a pond I was helping fix up before I went away. We were about a mile from the main road. The other to men with the team were after rock. I was there all alone. One came on a dead limb, a little wase from where I was. Such a concert for over an our. How is that for high? Some concert, believe me. I am pretty pleased to bee back in the country."

That was all! I have improved the capitalization and punctuation, but otherwise quote literally. Here was an elderly man whose even life had been interrupted by the most tragic incident that could come into his experience, and who, by a modern miracle, had been given a reprieve from what would have been a certain death sentence not so very many years ago. A judge of discernment, in an age grown merciful, had sent him home, requiring only that he write to the probation officer assigned to his supervision, and he had sat down, pencil in hand, in the frame of mind of a boy of six, seeking to correspond with a relative as a matter of Sabbath duty.

I read and reread this letter, until I wondered whether the shock of the murder had not killed the man James Benson and left only the boy Jim. It was cold in the little house, and he was waiting for spring. Spring reminded him of birds, and that fact recalled the thrush that he had heard sing. And he was glad to be back in the country again.

A month later a second letter came; and as I read it I surmised that Jim Benson had labored over it for hours before he found anything to say. "It is time to speak up and say something," he wrote. "I have been a good boy; at least I think so. I am at the same old job. I try to get things in shape, trimming trees and ceaping the house clean. Believe me, it is some job to ceap a house clean. Say, if you don't believe me, try it. I think you would say, right you ar, old man. I did not think years ago that it was a verry big job, but I have changed my mind. Thear you have it, strate from the shoulder."

I decided that it was my duty to visit Benson in his home. His state of mind was quite beyond me. But I was satisfied that keeping him in a cell would have accomplished nothing for him.

It was on a spring afternoon at the end of April, with the cherry and the early pear trees just coming into bloom, when I at length found time for the trip to his town. I had written to him to meet me at the railroad station, but I did not see him when the train pulled in, and I had started to walk up the country road before I discovered him waiting for me with a borrowed horse and buggy. In his cell at the jail awaiting trial, and again in the court room, he had merely suggested the taciturn man plucked from his own environment and set down amid unfamiliar surroundings. Jogging along now behind the old horse, with an unnecessary whip in his hand, I recognized the unmistakable type of the New England Yankee, probably less a farmer than a Jack-of-all-trades. A complete knowledge of what his life had been was necessary to me if I was to get a true line on his point of view.

We passed a village church, and I inquired, at a venture: "Do you go to church since you have returned to town?"

"Yes," he replied. "I didn't go for a spell once when we had a little tiff in the choir, but I go now."

"Sang in the choir, did you?"

"I led it for a time. I played brass horn in the band, too."

"And you were town constable. You must be considerable of a man out here."

"I was chief of the fire department for a spell," he admitted, not without pride, and flecked the horse.

This sketched in the background of his village life for me, and made me understand why the town had rated him as a good citizen. It was a sparsely settled community, in which every man must do his part; and Benson had not been lacking in public spirit.

We came at length to the home, a not unattractive house with ten acres of land; but the soil was run out and uncultivated; there were farm wagons in the shed, but no horses in the barn. The only signs of industry were a large woodpile at one side of the house, and a little one-room building at the rear, fitted up as a cobbler's shop.

"Homestead?" I inquired; for it suggested the run-down farm of a nearly extinct family.

"Oh, no," he answered. "Mother bought it when we were little children."

I thought that his voice faltered over the word mother.

"She has been dead several years?"

"A good many years."

"And you two boys lived here alone after she went?"

"Yes," he replied, and then with sudden vehemence added: "And I wish to God we had sold the house when mother died. Then this thing never could have happened. I was planning to sell it this spring and get out. I had the feeling for a long time that something was going to happen if we stayed here."

At last I was on the real trail of the tragedy. There had been a story that had not come out in court.

"But why did you remain so long?" I asked.

"It was mother's home," he said; and told me the whole story. All the pent-up flood of his memories seemed suddenly to break their bonds.

When the Civil War had reached the point where Abraham Lincoln was calling upon every able-bodied citizen to uphold the Government, Jim Benson's father went to the front. He left behind him a wife and four small children, the youngest but little more than a babe. And from that hour the woman was the sole support of the family.

When the news came of her husband's death in battle she moved from the city into the country, investing what little money she had in this home, and here, for several years, her struggle was a desperate one, though she never faltered nor lost her cheerfulness. She made all the clothing worn by her three

sons and her daughter. She braided the straw for
the hats that she fashioned for them. She raised
the meat and vegetables that they ate; gave them the
rudiments of their education at home, sought to in-
spire them with ambition.

Once son did go out into the world, and acquired
an honorable profession. The daughter was well
brought up, and made a good marriage, moving beyond their immediate circle. But the other two boys,
who had worked from the days of their childhood
in their efforts to meet the economic problem of the
family, and who had in the course of many occupations acquired the shoemaker's trade, remained at
home, and built themselves a tiny shop in the back
yard, which contained their two benches and kits of
tools. Jim tried at one time to branch out and become a milkman, there was so little money to be
made at the bench in competition with machine-
made shoes, but his brother remained at his task,
a slow, methodical worker, able to turn out only a
limited number of shoes a week, and to earn enough
for his bare necessities.

When the mother died the brothers, now grown to
middle age, undertook to run the house together,
sharing its expenses in common. The plan soon
went awry. Jim had considered himself the head
of the family, and had backed up his mother while
she was alive. Now he resented the inability of his
brother to pay his share of the taxes on the prop-

erty, and finally Jim took to living in the house as his by right, the brother entering only at night to sleep, and cooking his meals over a little stove in the cobbler's shop.

They quarreled for years before the final dispute that brought about their tragedy. Unable to cut loose and go out into the world, since they were bound by their poverty, they dragged out an existence that had but little in common. Had they tilled the land together, it might have yielded them enough income to provide some of the comforts of life; but they were not farmers, and the soil remained idle while they worked each in his own way, passing into their bedrooms in silence at night, Jim to a couch in the living room, his brother to a chamber above. At one period they did not speak to each other for four months; at other times they quarreled violently.

"But I always gave in," Jim told me. "I would say to myself, 'Now you mustn't let him make trouble.' And so I would back down. Even after I was elected constable I would let him have his own way. One of us ought to have left the place and gone away."

Before cold weather came on that year, Jim went to the woodlot and cut the winter's supply for his kitchen stove. His brother put off doing so, and when the weather changed helped himself to Jim's pile.

On the day of the fatal quarrel, Jim entered the little shop to get a pair of pincers, and his brother charged him with taking property that did not belong to him.   Jim promptly came back with the accusation that his own woodpile was being robbed. The exchange of words was short but bitter, and in the heat of his anger Jim virtually told his brother that the place belonged to him, and that the other was a trespasser.

"I went out of the shop to go to the woodshed, and when I returned he was standing outside waiting for me, his fists up, squared for trouble," he related, leading me to the spot where this scene had occurred.   "I knew then that the fight we had so long put off was coming, but I turned my back on him, and went into the house by the door here.   I had reached the sitting room when I looked back, and there he stood inside the kitchen door, the axe in his hand.   I grabbed my revolver from the table, and cried 'Hold' in a loud voice."

"But you went into the house to get it," I suggested.   "You knew then that you might shoot him."

"No, it was this way," he explained.   "A little while before there had been a murder in the town, and the head constable being away, they had come for me, and they had had some trouble in getting me out.   So I always went to bed on the couch now ready for such a call, with my flashlight, handcuffs and revolver beside me. When I saw him coming for me with the axe, I grabbed the revolver in this room, and as a constable would have done to any one, I cried 'Hold.' But he did not stop. I fired to scare him, and the bullet went into the wall. I fired again, right through the door over there. I fired a third time, and the bullet struck the floor. I don't remember clearly what happened after that. We were both in the kitchen and the axe fell to the floor, and he tried to pick it up. So I fired at him, hoping to hit his arm, and he fell right there, and when I saw that I had shot him, I knew that I must notify the doctor and the police."

He actually tried to do these things. Replacing the revolver on the table, lest the sight of it alarm the women whom he had seen at work out of doors on the next farm, he called to them to come to his assistance, but they were frightened and did not respond, though they sent a boy to give the news. He ran up the highway in search of a doctor, and when he returned, unsuccessful, both physician and constable were there, and he gave himself up to them, turning over his revolver as evidence in the case.

Jim Benson told me this story in complete detail, enacting every incident of the scene as he related it, and when he was done he stepped over to his couch, and from a box beneath it drew out a little kitten that had begun to cry, and sat down and fondled it, promising to give it milk when I was gone.

I looked about the room, its walls blackened now by his careless fires, its religious volumes in a book-case, his mother's old hand-worked motto, "Peace and Unity," where the brothers must have seen it every day.

"So you are living here all alone," I said, "cooking your meals in the room where your brother died, seeing his things day after day. Doesn't it get on your nerves sometimes?"

"I forget about what happened, and then I miss him," he replied. "I went into the shop the other day, and forgot that he wouldn't be there. I wish that he had let me alone. I wish to God that we had sold the house when mother died, and gone away. When mother was alive, she knew how to manage us all. But after she died—"

It came to this then, that unless we could prove to his own mind that he was guilty of a crime, we could not make him accept a punishment. And he was not conscious of guilt. For years he had seen this quarrel coming, and he had feared his brother, and driven to fight at last, he had defended himself with the nearest weapon at hand, mingling the office of constable with his own frightened personality, but never losing sight of the fixed idea that

he was justified in his action.   After all, wasn't it
a problem for the individual, rather than for the
law?

I turned all the facts over in my mind as he drove
me back to the station, seeking to add them up and
draw the proper conclusion.   The people whom we
passed, men and women alike, greeted him cordially.
Evidently they had not judged him a criminal.

"Why did you never marry?" I asked suddenly.

"Because of mother," he said simply.

Then I thought of the thousands of lonely men
and women living similar lives on our scattered
New England farms, and I reconsidered a resolve
that I had just formed.   It was never to tell the
world the real story of Jim Benson's troubles.   Let
the public think what it would concerning probation
for the man who had taken a human life; I knew
that he had been sentenced to a solitary life with his
memories, which sooner or later must sit in judgment upon him and exact penalty to the last drop.

But now I looked at the matter from another
angle.   I had been seeking to trace the course of
what we term crime back to its beginning.   And
is not resentment, slow anger and bitterness of heart
the breeding-place for evil thoughts that grow into
desperate action in the hour of their fulfillment?
There are other lonely farms where the seeds of
tragedy are being sown because property disputes
or fancied personal grievances have broken the sa-

cred ties of family and blood relationship. I determined to tell Jim Benson's story in the hope that it might find its way to those who would understand.

CHAPTER XV

THE BOY WHOM PROBATION DOES NOT SAVE

When the Court placed Benny Dodge in my charge one day, I believed that I had a case peculiarly adapted to the treatment of probation. He was seventeen years old, but undersized and undernourished. His mother was dead, and he shared a workingman's home with his father. The police had arrested him for larceny, but the evidence presented at the trial offered nothing more serious than the fact that he had gone with other boys and stolen candy and various articles of minor value. This data seemed quite sufficient to assure me that Benny, who would not have been taken for older than fifteen, had not been given a fair show in life. He was passing through a period of life when a youth needs the care of a woman in the home, the guidance of a strong father, and above all, nourishing food and clean clothing. All of these things had been denied to him by the force of circumstances over which he had no control, and it was not surprising that he had joined a gang and gone astray.

Neither the Judge nor the District Attorney hesitated at the disposal of the case. Benny was a type with which they had become familiar, and only his age had debarred him from being treated as a juvenile delinquent, which would have assured probation in the lower court. So I took him, and realizing that he was of the working age, but without occupation, set out to find employment for him.

It did not prove an easy task. As an applicant for enlistment in the army, he would have been rejected on sight as physically unacceptable. And the industrial world, I have discovered, is beginning to give the same appraising look when a young man seeks to enter its ranks. Shorter hours and better wages for workmen, compulsory compensation recovered for injuries received while at work, health regulations imposed by State inspectors, all have combined to place a new value upon the human material about to be engaged by the employer of labor. Benny Dodge did not look like a good risk. Men of quick decision shook their heads when I produced him before them and asked, in the name of good citizenship, that he be given employment.

But there must be a place for him somewhere, I argued; and at last I found it in a shop where five workingmen who had their dinner pails filled each day at a certain restaurant were willing to hire him to bring their noon meal to the mill gate.

This was not a job requiring special qualifications, and yet Benny fell down on it. His employers discharged him after a time because he was irregular in performing his simple duty. Men who eat from dinner pails have an appetite. They are accustomed to gratify it at three minutes, more or less, after the noon whistles have blown, and when the dinner comes a quarter of an hour late it upsets their schedule for the remainder of the day, and they get out of temper. The pails were always ready for young Dodge on time, but he sometimes failed to connect with them. That was my first intimation that perhaps I had a new problem on my hands.

I talked long and earnestly with the lad, and he agreed to find a new job, and report to me promptly. The months went by, but he failed to show improvement, and finally complaints began to come to me that he was loitering about the hallways of office buildings. I now began to study his habits more closely, and his defects became apparent. He did not arise from his bed until ten o'clock in the morning, and often had no food until noon, when his father returned and cooked a meal for the two. There are only a few men in any community who can cook and do housework successfully, and it is not fair to expect it from one who spends the day toiling in a factory. The boy was not receiving proper food; his hair was unkempt, his body dirty, his clothing unclean. It was no wonder that he did not have much of a hold upon his self-respect.

Eight months after the Court had given Benny

Dodge to me, I returned with him and asked that
he be sent to a corrective institution. "He has
committed no new crime, but I have failed in my
work because I am not making a good citizen out
of him," I explained. "He does not react to my
treatment. He needs some special assistance that
I can not give."

"Where shall we send him?" asked the Judge.

"We haven't the proper institution to meet a peculiar case of this kind," I admitted. "He ought to
go to our Industrial School at Shirley, but there is
an age limit there, and it barely excludes him. I
would recommend that he be sent to the Massachusetts Reformatory at Concord."

The Judge hesitated, and I could see that the District Attorney was inclined to frown. They did not
want to send up a boy who had not broken his probation; and there was another reason, perhaps. I
will be quite frank about it, for this discussion is
without value if it seeks to conceal anything that
throws light on the problem of salvage. There is
an opinion gaining headway in many quarters that
reformatories in this and other states do not reform; that our expenditure of thought and money
has somehow been in vain. I am not prepared to
say that it is an opinion always based upon personal
knowledge of the aims of such an institution, or the
details of its actual operation. Judges and prosecuting officers have ample work to keep them occu-

pied without making regular and frequent inspections of the places to which the wards of the State are sent, and their judgment in the matter is likely to be influenced by the fact that the graduates of reformatories and prisons return again and again to crime.

Nevertheless, there was no other place to which we could send Benny Dodge, and when I put him on exhibition at close range,—emaciated, listless, ragged,—Judge and District Attorney agreed, and he was committed to Concord. I did not intend that he should be mistaken for a criminal, and I telephoned to the superintendent, explaining the circumstances, and asking that if possible he be allowed to sleep in a dormitory rather than confined to a cell at night. But there was no dormitory available for such cases, and so he entered his new home with nothing to distinguish him from the other inmates.

There had recently come to the Reformatory as its official head a man of wide experience gained in other states, and he had succeeded a superintendent whom I had also known as a conscientious administrative officer and a man of high personal ideals. It occurred to me that if the Reformatory did not reform men under either of these officers, somebody ought to look into the system itself to discover whether the defect was in the machinery of administration, or in the raw product that it was undertaking to turn into finished goods. By sending Benny Dodge to Concord I had assumed a certain liability for the institution, because if it made damaged goods out of him, the blame would rest finally upon me.

But I left him there for several weeks before I paid my first official visit to him, and when I did go, I tried to put out of my mind the fact that I had often been within the great walled enclosure, and sought to look upon it as an intelligent plan to solve a vexing problem, and to discover to what extent it had failed.

Ideas and methods relative to criminology change from time to time just as medical knowledge progresses. I suppose that were this or any other state to begin the construction of a new reformatory tomorrow, it would purchase several hundred acres of land for the purpose, and construct its buildings on what is known as the cottage plan. But with state taxes always increasing, one can not scrap great institutions as battleships are discarded, and this fact must be given due consideration in seeking to get at the bottom of the unsolved problem of the undesirable citizen.

I recalled as I began my tour of the Reformatory that it was built originally as a new prison. This was in 1878, the year in which the old prison at Charlestown was abandoned; for all time, as it was then thought. Yet six years of experiment had sent the prison back to its old quarters, which were less liable to fire risk, and nearer to police aid in the unexpected event of rioting among the prisoners. It was then that this group of buildings, since enlarged, became a Reformatory, undertaking to teach useful trades to its inmates, the nucleus of whom were 117 prison inmates selected for that purpose.

These facts, of course, have very little to do with the Benny Dodge of today. My chief interest was to discover in what direction methods had improved in the three decades. Such improvement is to be noted in many ways. In the old days prisoners were treated in the mass; today they are considered as individuals. There is a building filled with shower baths, in which the 800 men are required to bathe regularly. There is a semi-military drill in the open air to assure the proper amount of exercise. Medical inspection is rigid; the food is nourishing; the library is large; there are schoolrooms as well as workshops. The animating idea today, in Massachusetts and in other progressive States, is to reconstruct criminals rather than punish them. The public has yet to gain this point of view. It is not yet aware of the fact that in Massachusetts we have already reached the point where, except for the more serious offenses, it is as easy to keep a man out of a cell as it is to put him behind the bars. For every guilty person whom we lock up, we now release one who could have found no escape a few years ago.

"What is the first problem of the man sent to you here?" I asked one of the Reformatory officials, a man who had been in its service almost from the beginning.

"To determine his physical and mental condition," he replied.

"And the second?"

"To teach him a trade."

"He comes as raw labor then?"

"Almost invariably he is an unskilled laborer."

"And the matter of his discipline?"

"That gives us less trouble than it once did."

Nothing had been said about punishing the prisoner for the crime he had committed.

Let us take up the matter of the trade for a moment. Here, likewise, the public is but vaguely informed, and very limited in its knowledge of what is termed "prison-made goods." A young man sent here may become a carpenter, painter, tinsmith, plumber, furniture maker, blacksmith, iron worker, engraver of metals, machinist, printer, or learn the several trades of a cotton or woolen mill; occupations, all of them, that will assure him a comfortable living when he returns to the working world.

All of these industries I saw in busy operation, turning out their finished products; but the whole series of shops was manned almost entirely by young men. Although the law permits commitments from fifteen to forty years of age, the average was actually twenty-one and a half years; the age that wins our victories on land and sea in time of war; the age of contest on our athletic fields; the age that courts and marries and demands its fair place in the business of the world.

Why, then, were these eight hundred men here? The definite answer was not to be found in their faces as they worked diligently at their several tasks. One could not have identified their crimes or determined the probable degree of their viciousness. Seen at their best, they were an average lot of young men in working clothes.

As I sought the solution, I came upon Benny Dodge, weaving cloth at a hand loom. He grinned a welcome when he saw me, eager to engage in conversation. Although I had taken him from the freedom of the streets and given him a cell for a chamber, he said that he was doing well, and liked his work. He was not the boy I had sent in, though still below the normal physically. The bathing, the clean if plain clothing, the regular hours and the necessary amount of food, were putting him into shape for a better chance with the world beyond the brick walls. Had a similar problem of environment brought the others here?

"How many of these boys come from broken homes?" I asked the official.

"The majority of them are from broken homes," he replied. "Probably 75 per cent. are from broken or defective homes."

He had made a distinction, and I asked him what he meant by the defective home.

"The one in which the parents do not set a good example, or are unable to cope with the problem of their children getting beyond parental control," he explained.

Later in the afternoon, as we stood in the yard and saw the young men march by for their open-air exercise, I began to sense in bulk the physical side of the problem of the broken home. As the bugles and the drums sounded on the green, the doors of all the workshops opened, and the inmates came forth in double column. Invariably the head of these columns marched with shoulders erect and sure step; and as inevitably the men who brought up the rear slouched and their footsteps lagged. Studying their faces and their steps with a new interest, it became apparent here as it had not been over the mill machinery and the work-benches, that a certain proportion of this entire population was sub-normal, and that its cure within the period of treatment, which might extend from twelve months to five years, was no simple task.

Benny marched past me with his head held studiously high as the best of them. When brought to the Reformatory he had slouched in and slumped visibly in the presence of the superintendent, his hat still upon his head. There had not entered his mind up to that time any clear idea of discipline or authority, but there was hope now that he had begun to understand order and responsibility.

"Is the real problem here physical or mental?" I asked at length. We could repair the physical defects of Benny Dodge in a comparatively brief time; but what of mental deficiencies?

"Talk that over with the resident physician," suggested the official.

The resident physician of the Reformatory is Dr. Guy G. Fernald, and I found him in a laboratory in the wing of an excellent hospital. He has held the office for several years, and was called to it from the well known McLean Hospital. He qualifies as an alienist, and various medical papers that he has written for publication indicate that he devotes much of his time to original research work, looking to the permanent improvement of this human material that comes to him for inspection.

"So it isn't a matter of hospital cases alone," I said, to draw him out.

His answer was so much to the point that we did not refer to the hospital again. It contained less than a dozen patients that day, all convalescent from minor ailments. Its work is merely incidental to the larger task of examining the eight hundred men who pass through the institution in the course of a year, to classify them and prescribe the special treatment that is required.

The longer we talked the matter over, the better did I come to understand that this was nothing less than a human laboratory, in which the hundreds of specimens were studied like so many curious and instructive insects. Do not misunderstand me by this. The man committed to the reformatory is hardly conscious of this analytical examination. It comes chiefly when he is about to return to the world, and believes himself strong enough to stand up against future temptations.

The initial appearance of a prisoner before the resident physician,—a man in his prime, friendly in speech and diplomatic in his manner,—drops him into one of five general classifications as to his mental and physical condition. If there is a serious defect in his body that can be remedied, requiring the attention of specialists, he may be sent to the Massachusetts General Hospital, in order that a handicap that may have contributed indirectly to his lawlessness may be removed. If there are indications of venereal disease, there is no hesitation in ordering for his benefit a remedy that costs $4.50 for a single application. For the hundred blood tests that are made each year, the resources of the finely equipped Harvard Medical School are commanded. Which is to say that these human derelicts, having done nothing to deserve well of

the State, receive the very best that it can give
them.

Nor does their medical supervision end with the
preliminary examination and the special treatment
that may be necessary. There is placed in the hands
of each young man, as he waits his turn in the
doctor's office, a frank, typewritten discussion of
sex problems; an honest, honorable appeal that
should have come from his own father, but that,
in our system of mistaken prudery, has seldom so
reached him. He is given simple instructions, in
printed form, as to proper breathing, as to the diges-
tion of his food, as to avoiding contagion in colds
and influenza; information even as to the care of
teeth and ingrowing toenails.

But the real examination of the man comes when
he is nearing the end of his term, and has applied
for a parole, and is about to appear before the
Parole Board. His record of behavior in workshop and elsewhere, and the gain that he has made
in weight since he entered the Reformatory, are
matters easily computed; but when he reënters the
laboratory of the resident physician for technical
observation, it is to obtain a classification that he
himself is not to see, and that is, indeed, carefully
guarded from public record. It is confidential information concerning him that is available only to
the Board and the head of the institution; not to be
used against him in the world outside, but to serve

as a guide in determining his chances of making a good citizen if released.

Dr. Fernald has made the statement in addressing a medical society that there is no such thing as a complete morality test. Nevertheless he has devised what appears to be a fair working model, and it is in use every day in his laboratory to test the moral responsibility of the men who have been "under treatment," and whom the world expects to see discharged from the institution "cured." It is a simple process, less intricate than a picture puzzle. In the course of the conversation with his subject, the physician gives to him ten strips of paper upon which are printed various acts, ranging from robbing a blind man of his pennies, to arson and murder. He is asked to arrange the cards in their proper order of consequence. It appears to be a very simple matter, but the action involves moral distinctions upon close questions. Five men of normal moral sense will offer very little variation. Five men whose moral sense is abnormal will make a hopeless confusion of the arrangement.

Then a test is made for classification on the basis of mental status. "It is of vital importance that we measure the desire for achievement," is the manner in which Dr. Fernald states his proposition. "It is practical to measure in terms of muscle fatigue and units of time the kinetic will of the subject who stands supporting his weight with the heels off the floor, since fatigue is rapidly, naturally and harmlessly induced in this manner."

In operation, such measurement is obtained by placing the subject upon a piece of apparatus that rings an electric bell whenever his heels sink to the floor level. A movement of a needle point up and down indicates at every moment the relative position of the heels, and spurs the subject on to maintain his position and not permit the needle to fall below the dead line set for standard.

"I tried this once as a comparative experiment," Dr. Fernald told me. "I selected twelve pupils from a training school in Cambridge, and then I applied the test to 116 prisoners, of a somewhat sturdier type and slightly heavier in weight."

This was interesting, because it was a comparison of youths within the institution with young men of about the same age who had never broken the law.

"And what was the result?" I inquired.

"The average score of the men on the outside was more than twice as good as that of the prisoners."

"Yet their physical strength was about the same?"

"Very nearly so; enough, indeed, to prove that the test was an index of mental quality."

"And the conclusion from this experiment?"

"A positive deficiency among the prisoners of those mental characteristics which make for success."

Now, indeed, we were getting somewhere.

"Then to decide whether or not an institution of this nature can live up to its name, we must know whether the individual prisoner is capable of reform," I said. "What do your tests show, in the total, as to defectives, and what proportion of the men who are here today are likely to return, or to be committed to some other institution?"

"Sixteen per cent. are defectives," he replied, and added: "If we were able to treat them under ideal conditions, they would be segregated on a state farm, there to remain for an indefinite period. All that we could expect from them under the best conditions would be to become self-supporting. Probably 50 per cent. of the population here is subnormal to the extent that we may expect periodic infractions of the law in the future."

"Then neither the State nor the Reformatory is to blame for these men who do not reform?"

He opened the door of his bookshelves and took out a pamphlet on "The Defective Delinquent Classification," an article originally prepared by him for reading before the Boston Society of Psychiatry and Neurology. A moment later, when he was called from the office, I opened it at random and my eyes fell upon this statement: "Our legislative and judicial systems assume that the guilty prisoner is responsible for his acts unless he is shown to be insane; whereas, in fact, the defective prisoner is only partially equipped for life, and because of a natural, not acquired handicap, has at best but a limited responsibility."

I pondered over that statement, but I knew, from my own experience, that it was true. But the world, broadly speaking, did not realize it, and was ready to seek almost any explanation in the absence of the real one. Indeed, it was not until as recently as 1911 that any State had accorded legal recognition of this fact, and Massachusetts was the pioneer in the enactment of legislation for the establishment of separate departments, in three of the penal institutions of the Commonwealth, for the reception of defective delinquents.

The resident physician returned and going to one of his laboratory drawers took out a box containing a large number of cards, bearing type-written memoranda. Somebody in authority had asked for information concerning a prisoner who had petitioned for his release.

"And this is the recorded result of the laboratory work?" I inquired.

"Stated in practical terms," he replied.

He offered me several of the cards, identified only by their numbers, and I read such comment as this:

"Morality at fault. Accidental offender. Illiterate on arrival, now writes and reads a little English. Is boyish and untrained in vice, but has been neglected in intellectual and moral training. Shot himself because he feared arrest."

"Morality at fault. Responsible delinquent. Rather erratic and scattered in his thinking and lax in his planning. Morally and physically hardly capable of working his way through a law school as he hopes to do."

"Morality at fault. Has neglected advancement for amusement since leaving school. Some force of character, and has had a good home training. Promising material for reformation."

"Mentality at fault. Truancy has deprived him of formal equipment. Home training has been neglected. Is tractable and industrially capable, but very ignorant and childish, but has not been viciously taught."

"Mentality at fault. Formally is inadequately equipped and intellectually is retarded. Mental age is not above nine. Industrially is unskilled labor."

"Morality at fault. Responsible delinquent and habitual offender. Is poorly equipped formally. Is acute but unprincipled. Offers excuses and shifts his ground to avoid disagreeable admissions and admits that he would lie if he did not think it would hurt him. Does not appreciate the difficulty of reforming a pickpocket."

"Then much of it goes back to the home," I said as I finished the reading. "The delinquent and the criminal are made there." It was a harsh statement, but the responsibility must be placed somewhere.

"It is seldom from the well organized home that we obtain our Reformatory inmates."

"And the root of the problem reaches down to the family itself?"

"Yes; and how are you going to solve it?"

That is the difficult question, after all. When you have run the criminal down to the bad home, you have opened Pandora's box once more, and out jump such devils as The Slum, Booze, Ill Health, Discouraged Poverty, Immoral Living; and you must begin all over again. I looked over the home records of a group of prisoners, and the succession of phrases that arrested my attention was:

"Father a drunkard and criminal;" "Mania for running away since a child;" "Father intemperate;" "Mother insane;" "Brother and sister feeble minded;" "Father a drunkard;" "Fair home but he abused it." So on through a long list. It was the defective home that produced the sub-normal child, later destined to become a burden to the State.

On the way back to the city I found myself in a seat on the railroad train behind a clergyman.

"What, in your opinion, is the white man's burden?" I asked abruptly, desiring to draw him into a conversation.

He looked at me kindly for a moment, and assuring himself that the question was not put in jest, answered: "To save the Chinese Republic and win it to Christianity. There is no greater field of labor in the world today."

I shook my head in disagreement.

"Well?" he inquired.

I answered him but poorly, after all. Benny Dodge's problem was on my mind, but I found that I could not phrase it properly. Perhaps it was indeed easier to reorganize the Chinese Government than to make over our own American homes.

CHAPTER XVI

WHEN PROBATION FAILS TO REACH THE GIRL

Marie Laverne had a drunken father, a weak mother, and a sister sixteen years of age, who followed her implicitly. Marie herself was seventeen; and it is her story that I am about to relate.

When her father's sodden career finally landed him in jail, efforts of church and probation officer having failed to keep him sober enough to support his family, Marie decided that she would leave home to manage her own affairs henceforth; and her younger sister went with her. The weak, discouraged mother protested feebly, but it did no good. The girls had come to hold their parents in silent contempt.

The Laverne girls hired a cheap room in a not over-critical quarter of the city, and after a time made the discovery that when one was good-looking and smartly dressed, and understood how to handle young men, it was no longer necessary to work in the factory. The real blame for the situation now developing should be laid at the door of the drunken father and the irresolute mother; but the punishment was to fall, in due time, upon the girls themselves. Their butterfly career was brief and hardly worth the while, for when the police began to note them walking the streets late at night, their names were sent into headquarters, and it was not many weeks before they were under arrest as offenders against the moral laws.

My acquaintance with them began while they were in jail awaiting trial in the Superior Court. It was for such girls as these that probation was intended, and if we permitted them to be sent away without at least one earnest effort to save them, then the system had failed to recognize its most important item of salvage. But the matter did not rest with the simple question of whether probation should be granted. Any social service worker will bear me out in the statement that the girl who goes astray at this age under such circumstances as I have cited is like flotsam in a whirlpool. Unless you can lift her completely from her environment and place her elsewhere in a steadier stream of life, she will be drawn under again inevitably. An arrest is sufficient to brand her as prey for the underworld, and the mark thus placed upon her increases her temptations a hundred fold. The "right sort of young people" now shun her; but another class persistently hunts her, offering her fellowship in its ranks.

I took these two girls on probation, and the younger one I returned to her mother; a frightened, bewildered girl, conscious of the brink upon which she stood, and anxious to return to the shelter of her home, poor and insufficient as it was. We may dismiss her from this narrative, because she is still under my care as I write, and there is every reason to expect that she has been saved.

But Marie could not be sent home to the mother whom she had neither trusted nor respected. There was a rebellious gleam in her eyes a moment after the Court had granted her release as a probationer, and I knew that the world with its white lights still called to her.

"You must leave the city at once and go to work somewhere in the country," I told her. "We will secure a place for you doing housework."

"I don't know anything about housework," she replied; and this is generally true of the girl who comes from the defective home.

"We will find a woman who will teach you. The wages will be small at first, but you will be kept away from the old crowd, and as the people whom you meet will know nothing against you, there will be every chance to make good."

I found a place for her in the home of a judge, her wage to be three dollars a week until the time when her training made her worth more. Both the judge and his wife knew that I was sending them a probationer, but they asked me for no details as to her story. They were willing to accept her on her face value. In my years of experience I have placed such women in the home of court officers and police officials; a fact of evidence as indicating that men who have to do with the enforcement of the law are often ready to aid those who desire to reform.

But Marie, after a week of service in this excellent family, begged to be permitted to go home on a visit to her mother and sister. She was lonesome to see them again, she said, if only for a single day. The request was granted, and she departed with the promise to return that night. In the evening she telephoned for permission to remain until morning. But on the morrow she failed to appear.

Of course I went in search of her as soon as her absence was reported, and I did not find her with her mother. She had gone to her lover instead, the obligation imposed by her probation thrown aside like a discarded garment. Freedom for her under these circumstances was out of the question. It did occur to me that marriage might offer a solution, but when I talked with the young man in whose company I found her, I discovered him to be a moral leper, so that it became still more imperative to put her beyond the reach of the city.

We have in Massachusetts a Reformatory for Women. There is such an institution to be found in every state; some possibly better, but many to my knowledge very much worse. The woman in the home,—the good woman, whom God has given the right kind of a home,—turns aghast at the thought of these prisons, and so retains the ignorance of her husband and father upon the subject. Perhaps it is well that this is so, for the less publicity that attaches itself to such institutions, the better for the performance of their work. Nevertheless, if we are to gain an understanding of the modern treatment of criminals, which is just now in the process of a far-reaching evolution, we must look in upon one of these prisons for women; and what state is more typical of the times than Massachusetts?

The Old Bay State is in many respects more of a frontier today than it was when John Carver, John Endicott, John Winthrop and their fellows established their colony here. Streams of immigrants are pouring over her borders from every part of the globe. Mohammedan women who wore the veil go uncovered among the tenements here. Greek women who had been taught that one must remain indoors as the price of a reputation, find that there is no such restriction here. Hebrew women whose ancestors have been true to their traditions since the days of Abraham, meet for the first time those of their own race who flout a too-rigid orthodoxy. It is the great mart of the nations to which they have come; the uncensored life of a free republic; and it is not surprising that there is a reaction from the class distinctions of the old world.

But in spite of the fact that some do go astray, womanhood in Massachusetts holds its own better than in some other seaboard States. The population of the state is over three and a half millions, of whom nearly a third are foreign born, and of whom three-quarters live in the cities; but the number of women under sentence at the Reformatory seldom goes above 350, and at times drops a hundred below that number. Of our 176,618 arrests for all causes in 1914, 12,144 were women, and the largest number in all prisons at one time was 765.

When a woman can not be saved by simple probation, there are four institutions to which she may be committed, the State Industrial School, if she still be below a certain age, the county jails, the House of Correction, and the Reformatory. The judge sent Marie Laverne to the latter.

And by so doing, you will surmise, it branded her a criminal, since the public makes no distinction among those who have served time. Technically this is so, but within the Reformatory itself the prisoner is no longer looked upon as a person committed for punishment. I had confirmation of this when I made my first call to inquire for Marie Laverne. Inadvertently I remarked that I hoped that punishment would bring Marie to her senses; and in reply a woman gowned in white fairly vibrated with the rage of her feelings.

"How can we hope to save these women when you men still talk of prisoners and punishment?" she protested. "They are all sick—sick in body and soul. No woman who is normal goes wrong. This place is not a prison; it is a laboratory, a clinic. You must look into its work from that point of view."

Now this woman was the superintendent, the official head of the Reformatory, and she had a right to speak. She was a married woman and a widow,—a mother as well as a widow,—and she had been called to this post after successful service in hospital and institutional work. She had gathered about her a staff of women likewise trained in social service; a corps of women who abhorred the old institutional type of smug, overbearing matron, and who would not engage an assistant unless she confessed to some altruistic interest in her calling.

"So you look upon them not as prisoners but as patients," I said. "But can they really be cured, even from that angle of view?"

"Don't misunderstand me," she replied. "We have not discovered any simple method of solving the problem. What I say is that we must not brand them as convicts, but rather classify them and then administer according to their needs."

"That assumes that breaking the law does not make them all equally bad," I said. "Yet we send here women convicted of murder, larceny, drunkenness, moral degeneracy. We have sentenced Marie

Laverne to live among them. How is the law to make these distinctions?"

"The law must come to it in time," she answered. "We have the proof here that there should be at least three classes, and that each one should be kept apart from the others. What chance is there for the woman whom we know cannot go straight in the world, and yet who is sent back there to fall again? Our problem is not only to save her from contact with others, but to save her from herself. Somewhere in the scheme of things there is a place for her, and if that place be a State colony wisely supervised, then we should provide it for her. Is not that so?"

It is so; but I desired to draw her out still further in the matter. Let me note here that Massachusetts has given this great institution entirely over to the management of women. Aside from the head gardener, there is no man among its forty or more officers and attendants. While we have differed in our opinions as to the right of women to vote, we have not denied them the opportunity to aid in the solving of our vexed social problems. And what they are doing in this one institution is completely their own, and worthy of our study as men.

"Why should we keep any woman from her freedom when she has paid the penalty of her offense?" I asked.

"Come over to the office," she said by way of reply; and we went, meeting there a slender, reliant young woman, likewise gowned in white, whom she introduced as the doctor, informing her that we had come to look at her charts.

They were large cloth charts, such as I had not seen in any other penal institution, and one's first impression of them was an array of circles and arrows, and rows of little houses painted in groups, each group of a different color. Gradually I made out that these typified the various places within the state to which a woman could be sent; hospitals, refuge homes maintained by religious organizations, jails, houses of correction, the Reformatory. They were more numerous than one would have guessed.

"You have them all charted," I remarked.

"Yes, and this woman has been an inmate of all of them."

Whereupon I looked at the chart with a new interest, and at the point of beginning, to which my attention was now directed. Here was a girl from a degenerate home, who had gone astray at the age of fourteen. Her career since then had included twenty-two court sentences in twenty-three years. She had been arrested for no less than seven offenses, and was now the mother of fatherless children, and a victim of cocaine and morphine. And she had brought with her as toll in her latest arrest a young girl whom she had broken in to the use of drugs.

"Had we taken her twenty-three years ago, and discovering that she was mentally incapable of going straight, placed her in a segregated colony of her own kind, we might have prevented the terrible trail that she has left behind her," said the superintendent.

So they were doing here, in their own way, what the resident physician was attempting at Concord, and they had worked out a system along their own lines. The woman who came to them was not treated as a criminal once she had passed into their keeping, but a sister sick in body and soul, to be prescribed for within the limits of the law. And that was the point at which the system broke, for they could diagnose, but they could not always order the cure. When they found the woman marked for evil-doing or crime, they could not retain her indefinitely, but must send her back to the world, and then wait for her return. Almost inevitably this occurred.

I expressed a desire to examine the record of other cases. Possibly the one just given to me was the exception, an isolated example of depravity, and therefore not to be given undue weight.

They were shown to me, complete in detail, but bearing fictitious names, since these human documents are never to be fully disclosed to public view.

The first was that of a girl twenty-five years old, born in New York, her father a drunkard who had abandoned his family. Here was the first defect, then, to be recorded in her history. The mother had gone to work in order to educate her daughter, thus further weakening the home environment. The girl had entered the high school, intending to fit herself for college, and had done good work in her studies until the third year, when she had joined a fast set of girls, one of whom had taken her to a house of ill repute. From this point her downfall had been rapid, until she had left school and gone to work. The new friends that she formed in the business world were no better than the old. She began to associate with a young man who had been a former classmate at school, and he frequently took her to a hotel where liquor was served to women. There she met a young woman of her own age, a very worldly person, who advised her to quit using liquor and take "dope" instead.

She accompanied this girl to her room and was taught the use of heroin. That was in April, and by September she was in its power, and forced to take it every day. A druggist supplied it to her regularly, though he must have known that he was contributing to her ruin with every sale that he made. Fortunately he was arrested after a time; but the girl, thus deprived of her source of supply, at once turned to cocaine; but the price of that began to advance, and fearful that she might commit crime to obtain the required money, she broke the habit, only to take up morphine when she learned that it was peddled illicitly. She had left home now, the better to conceal her habits from her mother.

Ponder these facts, you moral citizens who cry out in alarm at the discovery that your high school students are being debauched. At every step of her downward course this girl living in a Massachusetts city found snares set for her, though they were always in violation of the public statutes. Liquor sold to minors; drugs offered to young girls; fake hotels permitted to become the meeting place for those going astray.

In due season the police net gathered her in. She was placed on probation, but failed to reform. Arrest again, probation for a second time with no better success, and finally the Reformatory for an indeterminate sentence of five years. She had broken the social laws, committed larceny, and been found guilty of unlawfully having morphine in her possession.

"And what did you do with her?" I inquired, looking up from the record.

"Gave her normal living," replied the superintendent.

"Built up her physical body," added the physician.

They related how they had fed her hourly during the period in which they were helping her fight her craving for the drug.　They took me to the clean and sunny room, not a cell, in which she slept and spent her leisure time.　They conducted me through the workshops, in which they had selected an occupation best suited to her training, and they spoke of the Current Events Class in which she had found an interest in reading the history of foreign countries.

Then we went outside to see how the women obtained their exercise and recreation in the gardens and fields.　They wore divided skirts, and broad straw hats to shade them from the sun, and freed from the scrutiny of men, worked at their masculine tasks unconscious of observation, and willing to do a fair stint of work.　They were developing a plan of gardens and walks designed by a life prisoner, and they labored under the direction of a trim young woman who wore a khaki skirt and an inimitable hat; a woman whose enthusiasm in her work was contagious.

"The female gardener?" I suggested.

The superintendent smiled.　"The chaplain," she replied.　"The law requires us to have one, but we leave the religion of these women solely to the clergy of their various creeds, who come here to administer to them.　The chaplain is really the music teacher.   You should hear the women sing. It is very wonderful."

In the fertile farm lands some distance from the main buildings another group of women were working under the direction of one of the long term inmates, cultivating a field of vegetables.   On a little hill in another direction a third group of women were clearing and beautifying the little burial ground where those who have died unclaimed within the institution were at rest.   And there were the little graves of babies there.   Ah, the pathos of that spot.

Back once more in the office, I returned to a study of the case that had interested me.   A young woman of twenty-five,—and what an age of promise that should be!—ruined by the forces of evil in a state that prided itself on its laws, sent here in desperate need of treatment.   Would she be cured within the five years?   Were these laboratory scientists able to tell me whether or not their experiment would succeed or fail?

I put the question aloud, and silently they handed me their judgment, already recorded in the case: "Her general attitude has remained unchanged. She will keep up the method which she has found to pay in the world of commercialized vice.   The institution has failed with her, as she gives no promise of fitting into any community scheme."

"But not all women who come here are so?"

"No indeed," they told me. "Three in ten are brought to their senses, and we never see them again. Many of the others are derelicts, who would keep out of trouble if they could have supervision in their lives."

Yet only three in ten for complete salvage is distressingly low. Who is primarily responsible for the wrecking of our women? How far back in their own lives must we go?

I found the answer by a further study of the documents in this particular case. The father was "immoral, alcoholic, a notorious liar," and had deserted his wife before her child was born. His father before him had been addicted to liquor, and had died a suicide. The mother, a good woman, had sought as best she could to safeguard the girl against this inheritance, but she had failed. The church had sought for a time to guide her footsteps, but it also had failed.

It came down to this in the last analysis, that a girl inclined to weakness by inheritance found herself drawn to other girls and boys of similar tendencies, and together they were swept into the whirlpools of our city vice. The blame for their loss to the community was a divided responsibility; and a Higher Clinic might well lay it first to the men whose blood had been transmitted to her through their parentage, and second to a dormant public conscience that made it so easy a matter for the young to go astray.

I had brought Marie Laverne to this social laboratory, and I realized now that the best they could do for her was to determine how much of a chance for permanent cure she had, and then work for her physical and moral upbuilding. She would be treated, not as a criminal, but as a woman whose eyes had not yet been opened to the responsibilities of life. She would be taught in the schoolroom, instructed in a useful trade, given exercise and recreation, and supplied with nourishing food. But they could not guarantee to make over the eternal feminine in her. That was a matter in which she had the final verdict.

Nevertheless the fact remained that women themselves were seeking to meet this problem, and were putting their consecrated energies to its solving. The days of rigid, narrow institutional dealing with the question of fallen women were at an end, and strong, capable hands, directed by fearless, intelligent minds, were stretched out to seek and find every bit of salvage that could be rescued.

CHAPTER XVII

LUIGI SALVADORE IS PAROLED TO TAKE A BELATED CHANCE

Luigi Salvadore, sentenced to prison for a term of years, has been paroled. Long ago I had him as a probationer, but he did not make good, and I was forced to surrender him. He was committed to the House of Correction at that time; but it did not reform him. There came a day when a judge, listening to the evidence against him, and looking over his record, sent him to the State Prison, a formidable granite bastile in Charlestown, built more than a century ago of such granite as was used in the construction of Bunker Hill Monument, which is hardly five minutes walk away.

Parole is our latest bit of progressive legislation in Massachusetts in behalf of the prisoner serving sentence in the several corrective institutions. Under an act passed in 1911, which two years later created a Parole Board, the man or the woman who has served two-thirds of a sentence and who desires to reform may petition for release on good behavior. If the experiment proves to be a reasonable success,—and its advocates believe that it has justified itself already, though more conservative critics still desire time to check up its results,—it will mark another forward step in the science of criminology. Probation is a helping hand offered to a man upon the brink of his downfall. Parole is a hand stretched down to him after he is in the ditch.

In the case of Luigi Salvadore, for example, a prison guard who had studied him at close range was skeptical when I asked him whether the man had really repented.

"He said that he intended to reform, didn't he?"

"And very likely he does," I argued.

"But can he?"

"Why can't he?" I persisted.

The guard gave me an inquisitive glance. He was a typical prison officer, six feet tall, of powerful frame and in his prime, and he held the prevailing opinion that the majority of men were sent to prison because they could not keep out, and that the end of the world, however remote, would find about the same proportion of evil-doers.

"Look here," he said. "You know as well as I do how these people happen to be here. Except in rare cases of a serious crime, they are not first offenders, but old criminals. They have served time before in other institutions. In culling after culling, they have been left and finally have landed here. Is it reasonable to expect that they are going to be made over by letting them out on part time?"

"It will help reduce the cost of prison maintenance, and that ought to appeal to the public," I suggested.

"Oh, if you put it on that score, of course. Personally I have no opinion in the matter. I am here to do my duty, and I perform it without ill-will. But you asked me about Salvadore. He has been in here before. Why did he come back?"

Why did he come back? There was much food for thought in this question. What did State Prison in Massachusetts really do to a man after its grim steel gates closed upon him? The country had been hearing much concerning the reforms inaugurated at Sing Sing in New York and in various western prisons. Criminologists were busy warning us that our entire system of treating criminals was radically wrong. Luigi Salvadore was a typical criminal, who had resisted all efforts to remould him into a good citizen; was it possible for him to perform the miracle all by himself?

It occurred to me for the first time that these two granite structures in Charlestown, the prison and the monument, stood for two great facts in our civilization, both of them dealing with the individual. At Bunker Hill men had stood together for their rights in the face of death, and tens of thousands of patriotic Americans now made annual pilgrimage to the place where they fought. In the prison men who would not respect the rights of the majority were held against their will; and their number, in the century that had elapsed, many times exceeded all the Continental troops that had fought in New England. Yet the public did not come here. The prison was like a closed book, known only by its title. I did not feel competent to open it, and yet I desired to examine what Salvadore had found there, in order that I might determine his chances for redeeming himself on parole.

Aside from the frequent barred doors that arrest one's progress, this prison of eight hundred convicts is less suggestive of punishment than it was a decade or two ago. There have been no prisoners in stripes, no lock steps, no iron discipline in the workshops these several years. Massachusetts anticipates many of the reforms that are obtained only after exposes in other states, and thus averts more or less scandal in such matters. Critics of her institutions there always are, but violent reorganization of her administrative bodies is seldom necessary.

The warden of this prison has been in the service of the State for thirty-five years, and had been absent from his duties but three days in the twenty months preceding. As he sat in his office, the official head of nearly a hundred prison officers and clerks, one would hardly have guessed the nature of his business, unless from a glance at the volumes on criminology that crowded his bookshelves.

He was no theorist on the subject of prison reform, and held no false opinions concerning it. As deputy warden, and later warden, he had seen many thousand criminals at close range, and his conclusion was that the crimes that brought men to prison unfitted many of them from ever again being other than weak, unreliable citizens. He could give them a productive trade, and send them out in better physical condition than when they came in, but he knew what would inevitably happen to them. A certain number would leave the state, and word would come from them later that they had established themselves at an honest occupation. Others would soon fall into want, and reappear in institutions maintained for the physically broken or the needy. He would not lay down any hard and fast rule as to who were salvage and who were not, because the individual element was the final one in every problem. At best the life of a professional law-breaker was a short one, but the fact that there were only a relatively few aged criminals, did not of necessity indicate that there was a definite age of reformation.

I recalled the fact that a judge had once said to me, during a session of the court: "What becomes of the professional criminals? They must reform, because they do not come back after a certain age."

There is an age when the professional crook is too old to play the game successfully, and it comes comparatively soon. The excesses of his irregular life, the frequent terms of prison sentence, the natural burning out of the fires of his youth, bring him to a point where he no longer has the confidence that is necessary to his calling. He determines to incur the risk of detection and punishment no more; but his day of earning money honestly has too often gone by, and we find him later in an almshouse, or committed at his own request to the State Farm.

I wish that I might etch with the vividness of a Whistler the successive scenes that unfold themselves within a prison; not the unusual scenes that might be staged from time to time, but the everyday phases of the life to which men who have been sentenced by the Courts are committed. In the guard room on that afternoon of which I write sat a murderer serving a life sentence, spending the one coveted hour of the month with his wife. We sometimes depict crime upon the motion picture screen, when actors endeavor to portray the feelings of men behind the bars, but I wish that the face of that man, and the drooping figure of his poverty-pinched wife, might be shown just once in all the photo-play houses of the land, so dreadful were they in their unconscious pose of lost hope. He was a man still under forty, so that he should have many years to live, but the light had gone out of his eyes, and at the end of a quarter of an hour speech had already failed him, though the faded wife, in her garments that were four years out of fashion, was doing her best to turn over the exhausted topics of their conversation. And it was not the State that punished him. He was living better than murderers have fared at any time since the beginning of the Christian era; but the spirit within was torturing and chastising him, and I surmise that no ancient instrument of punishment could have caused him greater mental anguish than the sight of this woman, condemned with him, though free, to suffer through the years.

I left them, for the guard with whom I had spoken concerning Luigi Salvadore was about to conduct a group of visitors through the prison, and I desired to accompany them, to gain their point of view. We passed into one of the wings of the building where there were five tiers of cells, all of them open, for their inmates were at work. A century ago, and these cells were half their present size, mere tiny dungeons cut, as it seemed, in the solid stone, often damp and always poorly lighted, with only a plank for a bed. But as we passed them now, they were not unlike the little staterooms on the older trans-Atlantic steamships. Each room had its bed, table, chair and small cupboard. There were pictures upon the walls; usually framed illustrations from the magazines, but occasionally pho-

tographs of members of the family at home.   And
in almost every cell there were laid out for sale
articles made by the prisoners in their leisure moments; canes, toy canoes, frames, leather purses, oil
and water color paintings, manuscript music,—a
variety sufficient to suggest the familiar booths of a
beach resort.

One of the visitors, a rotund little man with efficient respectability personified in his well-groomed
figure, paused at the end of the corridor and gave
utterance to thoughts within him that suddenly demanded expression.

"Here is the beginning of trade and barter," he
explained, addressing us all as his audience.   "Human activities are often directed to no purpose in
the world at large.   But lock up a given number
of men, average men,—bad men, if you will,—and
they begin to produce articles of use to the race,
though they never did so before.   That is how civilization got its start."

"These are not bad men," retorted the guard, the
lines of whose mouth seemed to express scorn of
the comment of the world as he heard it in these
prison rounds.   "These are men like you and me,
only they got caught.   Except for the cranks, whom
we have to watch, there is nothing especially strange
about them."

He indicated the register of inmates that is posted
on the wall of each corridor, not unlike the member-

ship lists that one finds at his club. There was every manner of name there, from the New Englander down through a dozen nationalities.

A group of favored prisoners scrubbing the stone floors caused the rotund little man to change the subject and inquire as to whether there was much sickness in the prison. This was a pertinent question, because one hears so often of a man entering upon a long sentence, only to obtain release through death from tuberculosis, or be pardoned out to die.

Yet the rate of death and the amount of sickness among these men is no greater than among a corresponding number of men in the world outside, of similar antecedents. The life is more regular than the average one among them has known before, and those upon whom the confinement begins to tell are given work in the open air rather than in the shops. A rigid inspection of the eight hundred men a short time before had disclosed but four cases of incipient tuberculosis, and these had been removed, and their cells disinfected. Naturally dissipation has planted the seeds of disease in the bodies of many of these men, and confinement does not retard their growth; but it is no longer the prison of itself that condemns them to a short life.

We passed through the kitchen, where a dozen men were taking loaves of bread and pans of gingercake from the ovens, and others were cutting meat for the next meal, and began our inspection of the workshops. What always claims my attention at such a time is the obvious fact that these workmen might be at their tasks in any factory or shop room. Aside from the officer and instructor in each room, there is little suggestion of the nature of the institution, so that the rotund citizen was forced to remark as we passed from the shoe-shop to a room in which furniture and beds were being made:

"I supposed that in prison one made only shoes, and I had pictured the shops as having armed guards all about. Isn't it here that trouble usually occurs?"

"There is seldom any trouble now, for we don't nag the men," the officer of the prison replied. "We just treat them like ordinary men. Then the new parole law has helped discipline some, for the men want to get out, and they have to cut out hooting from the cells, and that sort of thing, to be eligible. As for the trades, there are a number of them."

I thought of Luigi Salvadore. He had lived from hand to mouth,—or more literally, from hand to pocket,—during his checkered career, and he must have stood in need of an instructor when he found himself set to a lawful occupation for the first time.

"What is a man worth as a trained workman when he leaves here?" I inquired.

"There are men in the shoeshop who could make their $30 a week outside," answered the guide.

"And the carpenters?"

"They are demanding $25 a week for a five-day week in Boston at the present time, I believe."

"And the hosiery workers?"

"Some of the largest hosiery mills in the country are to be found right in this state."

"Then a man who wanted to start honest again could soon get on his feet in the world?"

He gave me a look of pained surprise. "Say, we put the chance right in his hand," he replied; and burned up what other words might be in his mind with a completely withering look.

Then we went to the school-rooms. I remembered that the warden had reminded me that this had been the first prison to introduce education as an element in reform, but I was not quite prepared for the large room filled with chairs and desks, each one of them occupied by an adult, and the equipment of blackboards and maps and books upon all sides. The men in this class were the illiterates, or those who could not read and write English when committed; and here they were, being taught by educated prisoners, and learning with an eagerness that involved no matter of discipline.

"We have a hundred in the beginners' school,

and three hundred taking the correspondence course," explained the guide.

"Then many of these men may have fallen into crime through ignorance," I suggested. Luigi, for example, though very deft with his fingers and very sharp with his eyes, had not employed them for writing or reading.

"Rot!" replied our guide, with fine emphasis. "We have college graduates serving time here. One of them is in our school studying Spanish and Italian. Education has nothing to do with crime one way or the other."

As we left the school-room an Italian, a man of perhaps thirty, was reading aloud to the class the story of Abraham Lincoln's early efforts to obtain an education. He read with eager enjoyment, and his most earnest hearers were five Negroes, who listened with an odd look of response in their faces, as though the name Lincoln had sounded a dim echo back in their own childhood.

"And these are the worst criminals in the state," I remarked as we crossed the yard again.

"The worst, and representing every crime on the calendar," the guide agreed.

"And the old theory of treatment was repression."

"While to-day fifty per cent. of them find expression in the school courses alone," he added.

Returning to the prison office when the trip of inspection was completed, I said to the warden: "When a prisoner is discharged you give him a new suit of clothes and a few dollars in money, in addition to what he may have had when he came here. But what becomes of him when there is no friend waiting to meet him and take him home?"

"He goes to the State House at our suggestion and reports to the agent whose duty it is to aid discharged prisoners," he replied. "You must have been there ere now."

Of course I had, but I went again, still in the spirit of an inquiring public, in order that I might weigh the chances of Salvadore becoming a law-abiding citizen once more.

The agent referred to, George E. Cornwall, has his office in the suite occupied by the Prison Commission, and in his twenty-four years of service he has gained a personal acquaintance with fifty thousand criminals. The majority of those who leave the various state penal institutions report to him, and receive, according to their needs, board money to start them anew, additional clothing if the season requires it, tools if they desire to enter a newly acquired trade, and car-fare if they wish to go to a more distant city. They may even return to him a second time for aid; and the disbursements run into thousands of dollars each year. To this office Luigi Salvadore had come, having acquired a trade, the rudiments of an education, a commutation of sentence, and financial assistance to maintain him until he found employment. What more could a State established by the God-fearing, law-abiding Pilgrims be expected to do for him!

"They do not all make good?" I inquired as a matter of form.

"No," Mr. Cornwall replied, in the same spirit.

"But some of them really reform?"

"They do when they have convinced themselves that crime does not pay."

"Then we do not convince them from the outside? Real reform must come from within the man himself?"

"Always from within," he agreed. "We often aid men who are so broken by age and their experiences that they dare not risk crime again, but they are not really saved, and such men soon become public charges in some other form."

"But tell me of one real case where you know that a man has been saved from within; where he has become a self-respecting, productive citizen again."

He mentally reviewed his recent cases for a moment, and then he said: "There was a man named Leavitt, who is working in Boston now. He came to me two years ago from prison, and he remarked: 'If I knew of a job where I could honestly earn $10 a week, I would give up this life for good.' He was a man of thirty-four years, and he had served many sentences.

" 'If you really mean it,' said I, 'I will help you.'

" 'I really do mean it,' he replied, and he spoke as though he did. He had been a printer in his younger days, just an average printer, and I found a job for him wiping presses. He offered to take the job at $10 a week, but wages had advanced while he was out of touch with the world, and they paid him $13 to start with. He has worked for the same company for two years now, and his weekly wage at the present time is $30. I have some of his savings locked up in this office at this moment. There is no likelihood that he will ever go astray again, because he has figured out in his own mind that it is more profitable to go straight than it is to play the other game."

"That is the real problem, isn't it; to make the man who has become a social outlaw figure out for himself that the game will beat him in the end?"

"That is just it," he replied. "We may give him one more chance, whether it be by probation, parole or pardon, but salvation itself must come to him from within."

Good luck to you, Luigi Salvadore! May you read and understand these lines.

CHAPTER XVIII

THE MYSTIC APPEAL TO THE UNSEEN GOD

There came a day when a woman entered my office on an errand that was to reveal a phase of the criminal problem that had not occurred to me up to that time. She urged me to recommend for probation a young burglar of unsavory reputation, in order that he might be turned over to her for treatment, and she said that she had come in the interest of his family, who were excellent people.

"What is your profession? How do you propose to treat him?" I inquired.

"I am a Christian Scientist, and I believe that we can save him," she replied.

Now it chanced to be a case with which I was familiar, for the burglar had been examined by alienists and found to be insane, and had been transferred to an asylum that very week. I informed her of this fact, deeming it sufficient to dismiss her request; whereupon she quietly but firmly asked me if there was any way in which she could undertake his treatment there.

Of course there was not. When the law begins to take its course with a man, it is not for the private citizen to prescribe, however good the intention may be.

"And do you realize that you are asking permission to perform a miracle?" I added.

"Yes," she replied. "Our church, whatever you may think concerning it, has been built upon miracles."

After she had gone away, unsuccessful in her mission, I sat down and began to ponder the mysticism of what her words meant. In an age when a great many men deny the possibility of miracles, in a day when not a few moderns are inclined to reduce the soul to some form of mechanics, this woman believed that the worst of beings, the depraved criminal, could be saved from himself through the power of God.

I am frank to say that I did not take this matter up for discussion with the judges or the lawyers with whom I came in daily contact. This question of the soul is almost a private matter, and one must go about it discreetly, if not furtively. But I did begin to make cautious inquiries among the men who came to me on probation. In nearly every case I knocked at a closed door, as it were. Only one man confessed to me that once, hard pressed by his crimes, he had gone to the church in Boston where the Emanuel Movement was attracting public attention, in the hope of being saved from himself. Nothing had come of it.

But even if nothing had, the fact was worth noting that this man, irreligious and profane, had not gone beyond the pale of mystic belief. I determined, when the opportunity offered, to take up this question of a prisoner's soul, in the hope of learning whether or not it entered into his ultimate salvation. An odd thought, that, and yet I could not find that many books had been written concerning it.

Harold Begbie, in his "Clinic of Regeneration," cites case after case in detail where the criminal, while at large, was reached by the Salvation Army and finally brought to his knees repentant. But that was in the London slums, outside of prison. There is no record of its having been made an official part of the treatment of a prisoner within a corrective institution.

The months sped by, and in the pressure of other work I gave no further attention to this matter for a long time. Indeed, it was not until a chance reply to my question as to how many agencies within the Reformatory were exerting a real influence among the prisoners, including the resident physician and the chaplain, that it occurred to me that in my personal acquaintance with the latter, I had never sat down with him and asked to know the personal, private matters of his work.

And so, on the following Sunday, I attended service in the Reformatory chapel, to gain the proper background for this investigation. The congregation numbered several hundred men, for though it was not compulsory, nearly all of the prisoners attended, irrespective of creed. They sang familiar hymns to the booming invitation of a pipe organ played by a woman, and they sang with unexpected spirit.

Nor was this all. In the choir seats were thirty male singers, and when the time came for the first anthem these men arose and sang the beautiful composition containing the words:

"Vouchsafe to keep us this day without sin."

It was wonderful singing, so rich in its volume, and so expressive in its appeal, that I wondered what would happen could these men be transplanted, for a Sunday, to any of our great city churches, with their identity not disclosed. I will venture that more than one person in the congregation would offer the comment: "There is a choir of consecrated singers." And they were young fellows doing time! But were they not also men whose response to the call of anthems and hymns might disclose to me that odd bit of mechanics called the soul!

It was during the afternoon that I talked the matter over with the chaplain. His sermon had not given me what I wanted to know. It had been a simple address to the prisoners that began with the statement: "I don't believe that any fellow ever aspires to become a coward and a liar." It was an appeal to the better side of a man as against his "yellow streak"; but there was no mystic call for conversion in it, no offer of miraculous salvation from a man's sins.

"And as chaplain I can not do that," he explained. "We have here Catholics and Protestants and Jews. We have many faiths and creeds, and the State of Massachusetts does not place one above another. In all my years of administration here I have never told a man to do other than live up to the religion of his fathers; I have never preached my own church to him."

The chaplain at the Massachusetts Reformatory is the Rev. Robert Walker, an Episcopalian. He was pastor of the Church of the Ascension in Cambridge at one time; was chaplain at the House of Correction in East Cambridge for a term of years; served as a member of the School Board in a district where his own political party was greatly in the minority; a good mixer in the world, and not afraid of men.

It is his duty at the Reformatory to examine every man committed there as carefully as the physician looks them over; he for spiritual defects rather than physical handicaps. He asks the prisoners about their early religious training, advises them how to conduct themselves while in the institution, inquires as to what books they have read, and puts them in touch with a library of six thousand volumes that includes no less than eleven copies of "The Life of Lincoln."

"And after the preliminary interview, you see them from time to time in their cells?"

"Whenever they need me."

"But you never talk religion to them?" I asked.

"I try not to give them any theology," he answered.

"But there must be times when their souls do trouble them," I argued. "What do you do then?"

He told me this story. A few days before one of the boys had been sent to the hospital for an operation that might prove fatal, and his mother was notified of the fact. She did not come to see him; indeed, she had been indifferent concerning his fate since the day of his arrest.

But the chaplain went. He told the boy how close he was to death, and added: "Don't you want me to say a prayer for you?"

"Yes," replied the boy, his eyes expressive of more than his spoken word.

"Or better still, you repeat the Lord's Prayer," suggested the chaplain. "Then it will be your own prayer."

The youth hesitated for a moment. "I never learned the whole of that prayer," he said slowly. "You will have to say it with me."

The chaplain began to pray at his bedside. The lad joined in the opening sentences, and then broke down. It was necessary to teach him the world's most familiar prayer.

"What country had he come from?" I asked.

"He was a native of Massachusetts," was the reply. Once again I had come upon the product of one of our defective homes.

The chaplain related a second story from his experiences. It occurred while he was serving at the House of Correction. In the hospital there he found a man seventy-five years old, who had been a successful criminal for sixty years. Just consider, for a moment, what that means. Criminals are almost extinct at such an age, and a man who has had no other profession for sixty years is not to be found among ten thousand prisoners.

Looking the aged convict over with a scrutinizing eye, the chaplain saw that he had not much longer to live, and that the time had come when he might properly ask him whether it was well with his soul. He did so, and was promptly rebuffed. The old man looked him in the eyes scornfully, and said ironically:

"You can't talk to me about God or prayers. I haven't any use for either of them."

"Um!" said the chaplain. "How about Bartlett pears?"

It was in the winter, when almost no fruit was in season. The old man's eyes glistened. "What do you mean by Bartlett pears?" he demanded.

"I know where to get a jar. They taste like the real thing. I will bring you some from Boston to-morrow."

The Commonwealth does not provide canned pears at seventy-five cents a quart for its prisoners, but the chaplain produced them on the following day. He had opened negotiations for this aged sinner's soul, but by a route that his man did not know. It is frequently so in these prison conversions.

The object of his interest grew weaker day by day, yet with the same scorn of death that he had always shown to the law. Then, quite unexpectedly one day, when the clergyman called, he said with a strange look in his eyes: "Say the Lord's Prayer."

The chaplain prayed, and looked up from the prayer to a changed man with shining eyes.

And then this man who had lived in crime for sixty years told the story that he had kept hidden for more than half a century. As a boy he had committed a misdemeanor and been sent away for a time as a punishment. He had admitted the justice of this, and while locked up had come to a realization of his wrong-doing, and had determined to make amends when he returned to his home. Yet his former mates received him coldly when he sought to rejoin them. A mark had been placed upon him because of his arrest. He went back to the Bible class to which he had belonged; and they looked upon him there as one committed to sin.

"I resolved never to go to church again and never to utter another prayer, and from that day to this I have kept my word," he said. "I have denied God, and kept away from his people."

"And after you had prayed?" I asked the chaplain.

"He was another man."

"He had made his peace with God?"

"That was the phrase we once used. Now we are likely to say of a man, 'He thought things over.'"

"Why should we be expected to save them?" asked the chaplain later. "The church has failed. Society has failed. Even civilization has failed to make them good citizens. Why should they expect us to become such specialists that we can turn out reformed men from such material as we have here?"

He did not make the comment bitterly, but seriously. The problem is a larger one than the law-abiding citizen realizes. Yet the latter, being the tax-payer, is the one who expects immediate results.

"Why should a man from a bad home, below par mentally and physically, without a trade, want to seek God here?" he continued. "As a matter of fact, it is only the older men, and those who are soon to face death, who ever give serious thought to these matters."

"Then men who have committed great crimes do face God before they enter the electric chair?" I inquired.

"I will tell you the story of John Schlidowski," he replied.

John Schlidowski was a Polander who had murdered his wife. It was one of the most brutal crimes of a decade, and the man merited nothing but death. He had killed a woman whom he had married because she had saved a few hundred dollars by her own labor, and having put her out of the way, he had planned to go to California and establish himself to better advantage; but the law had intervened.

To this man, in his cell awaiting a trial certain to convict him, came the chaplain, with the usual offer of his office, and straining his face against the steel bars that separated them, the murderer said in reply: "I am an infidel and atheist, and I will have nothing of your God, your Christ or your Church."

"All right," the chaplain answered, unangered. "I have no God, no Christ and no Church for you. I have no Bible; but I thought that you might like

a primer.   You do not speak English well, and there
is a chance to learn it while you are here."

John Schlidowski thought that this was a good
idea, and said that he would willingly learn, since
he had a good education in his own language.   The
book was obtained, and the chaplain began his in-
struction.   There was never a word of religion or
repentance in all the teaching.

But on a certain Sunday night the chaplain found
the prisoner in tears.   He said that he had been
reading a story that made him think of his own life.
It was a simple story, and to this effect: A boy
started for the fields to gather berries.   His father
advised him to sit down by the first berries that he
found, and seek his fruit there.   He did so, but
when a number of his companions passed by they
laughed at him for being satisfied with such small
fruit, because they said that larger berries were to
be found in the fields just beyond.   The boy did not
heed them, but remained where he was, and when
they returned empty-handed late in the afternoon,
his own pail was filled.

"And so it was with me," said John.   "I had a
wife, a home and work, but I had heard that more
money was to be made in California; and here I am
empty-handed, with my life nearly gone."

That was the beginning of John Schlidowski's
awakening.   He had denied God and soul and conscience, and thus made secure against the future, as

he supposed, had feared no retribution. But now a force within him, not dead, though so long stifled, was rising to call him to judgment.

On Good Friday an unknown woman left at the home of the chaplain a box of luscious fruit, with the request that it be sent to the murderer. It is hardly probable that she knew the Polander or had ever seen him. There is a strange sentiment prevailing among women of a certain leisure class that sometimes brings them forward at such a time. When a murderer who had been born in a poorhouse, and who had never risen in life, went to his death a few years ago, he received a beautiful box of violets from a society woman who would have scorned to know him in private life. Condemned men have received original poems and personal gifts upon more than one occasion.

Quite familiar with this inexplicable practice, the chaplain took the box of fruit to the man, and said in giving it to him: "Somebody has sent you a Good Friday gift, though as an unbeliever you may not know the significance of the day."

"It was the day on which bad men killed Christ," John replied.

The following Sunday was Easter, and a friend sent to the chaplain sixty potted lilies. After they had been used in the chapel decorations, they were distributed among the cells, and one of them was left with John Schlidowski. Late in the afternoon an officer, passing his cell, discovered the man upon his knees in prayer. From a Boston newspaper given to him that morning he had made a series of cones, each of the many pages being turned to that purpose, and these had been fitted together in the form of a cross, which he had spread upon the floor of the cell. At the head of this cross was the Easter lily; and at the foot the murderer, seeking his God for pardon.

The chaplain, brought to this scene, did not disturb it. The man was of another faith than his own, and a priest of the Polish church had sought in vain to obtain an interview with him. The clergyman suggested now that this priest be called; but John would have none of it, neither then nor later. He himself had denied God, and he alone must again find Him.

"And he found Him?" I asked the chaplain.

"For a long time after that he found no forgiveness," he answered. "The trial came on, and he was adjudged guilty and condemned to death. He then passed through such a hell as I never want to look upon again. There could be no greater punishment thereafter inflicted upon him. Death itself was more merciful than what he endured in those days. He wasted away in torment before our very eyes."

Let me make these details very clear, for here is a bit of human evidence such as one is not often privileged to obtain. This infidel who had denied God and later sought to find Him, having restored the function of his conscience by this very act, now realized his crime as a terrible load upon his shoulders. The murder stood between him and his Christ; and the more he prayed, the greater became his suffering. There were days and nights of anguish in which he tore his clothing and his bed covering into shreds. He shrieked and moaned until a fellow murderer, condemned like himself to die, begged to be removed to a more distant cell because of the terror that this poor sinner inspired in him. He wasted away until his body was a mere shadow of its former self. He permitted his hair and beard to grow, until his image became one that to this day is stamped upon the memory of those who came in contact with him.

"There are murderers who die without a friend in prison," the chaplain told me. "There was such a one in prison at this very time, whose heart had undergone no change, and who evoked no sympathy among us. But this man's suffering was so terrible, and he sought so earnestly for peace, that we came to feel a personal interest in the outcome, even with a full knowledge of what his crime had been."

The chaplain visited him daily now, and as the time of his death drew near a new terror came upon the man. If he went to the execution chair without the knowledge that God had forgiven him, then there was no hope for him in the hereafter, and he was doubly condemned.

To save his life in order that his death might be accomplished as the law decreed, it was necessary at last to take Schlidowski to the hospital, and feed him there with liquid food. He no longer desired to eat. The body had given up under the terrible flagellations of the spirit.

"And one day in the hospital, as I went to his bedside, he seized my hands and drenched them with his tears," the chaplain continued. "IIe kissed them a hundred times, and he begged me to say the Lord's Prayer in his behalf. I did so, and he bowed his head in absolute devotion. I had talked morals with him, but never mentioned God, because I had told him in the beginning that I had no religion for him. Now, having sought in vain to find God alone, he turned repentant to the church. I prayed, and he repeated the words after me."

In that hour he found peace. Ten days before his execution he asked that something be read to him from the Bible. The chaplain recited the familiar Twenty-third Psalm. At the words, "Yea, though I walk through the valley of the shadow of death I will fear no evil," the condemned man interrupted.

"Read that again," he begged. It was the message that he sought.

As the day itself approached, it became urgent

to have the man's hair trimmed, lest the death current fail to work mercifully. Then he told why he had thus far refused to allow the barber to visit him. He remembered that Christ had worn his beard and hair long upon the cross, and he desired so to die.

In the hour of his death he walked calmly to the chair, asking only that the chaplain, the visible form of the Church, go with him and stand where his eyes could look upon him at the end. There had been final prayers in his cell, and on his way to the execution he spoke his last words. His lips were murmuring, and the clergyman asked whether there was anything that he desired to say.

He gave a negative reply with his head. "Chaplain, I pray often, lest I forget God," he said.

They adjusted the straps. The signal was given in silence, and the death current was turned on. The blue flame circled the forehead of John Schlidowski like a crown of thorns; and in that instant his spirit went forth to meet its God.

A miracle? No more so than the death of the thief upon the Cross!

CHAPTER XIX

TEN WOMEN WHOM PROBATION SOUGHT TO SAVE

A Master from out of Nazareth once faced a group of angry men who resented the intrusion of a sinful woman into their presence. We are very prone to condemn the fallen woman whose degradation becomes obvious beside iniquity that is not visible. Public opinion upon that remote occasion sentenced the Magdalene to be stoned, and the Master seemingly approved, but with the single reservation that he who was without sin should cast the first stone.

Sometimes, as I have seen the dragnet of our police system bring up from the whirlpools of city life the tragic, sordid women of the Underworld, I have remembered that far-away day when the Master rebuked mankind, and have wondered just where, in the final reckoning, the blame of besmirching womanhood will be laid. For of a surety vice as we find it in the world is not the initial work of women. They do not legalize the saloon, or invest their money in the barroom, or conduct the hotel of questionable resort. When they have been ruined, one may find them, it is true, sometimes in charge of the brothel, or recruiting for vice in its varied forms; but an honest judgment must seek out the original cause. It must go back to the man, or the man-made conditions, that robbed the girl of her innocence, and so made of the woman the thing for which nature did not intend her.

As I look back upon the many years of my experience as a probation officer, there is one day that still stands out vividly in my memory, though more than a decade has since passed, for it left upon my hands the gravest responsibility of any single day in court.

It was at the October session, when the legal world had returned to its tasks after a summer of recreation and rest. Unfortunately no such recuperation had occurred in the ranks of those who keep the courts in business, and as the late Justice Bond looked over the docket of prisoners that day he saw before him ten women, nine of them up on appeals taken for sentences imposed by the lower courts for drunkenness, all with records of previous arrest, and one an offender against the moral laws. The judge looked at them with whimsical inquiry for a moment, as though the trailing of countless drab women through his professional life had at last raised a question he could not answer, and then he said abruptly:

"Mr. Probation Officer, why is it that so many women come before the courts of our manufacturing cities charged with drunkenness?"

This question had occurred to me before, and I had sought to gain some light upon it. I informed him that seven of the women before him worked in the mills of our factory cities, and that of the ten only two were native born. In looking into the conditions that brought them to intemperance I had come to the conclusion that the drink habit was largely the result of lonesome lives and the lack of a home. Such women had often come from humble homes across the sea, but nevertheless parental roofs that afforded them traditional protection, for which they had since substituted the crowded boarding house, with its impersonal seat at a long dining table, and its sleeping room usually shared with another woman. Some of the older women had become addicted to snuff, which is a mild intoxicant when rubbed on the teeth and gums, and one that leads naturally to alcoholic drink. I made this statement as applying to general conditions. I was yet to learn of the individual temptations of this special group.

The judge scanned the records before him, intent upon some solution of the problem, which he stated tersely in these words: "Most of these women have served time in the Reformatory at Sherborn. It has failed to reform them."

I admitted that this was true. The State was doing its best at Sherborn; but it was not saving all the women sent there.

"Will you take these ten women on probation?" asked the judge, putting the problem up to me. "I want it done as an experiment. At the end of one year you may furnish me with a report on each case, bearing upon the probationer's conduct for that period."

I looked at those women, and I turned my face back to the judge, and I wondered whether he realized the task that he was imposing upon me. Six of the women, who had been free for a time under bonds awaiting the retrial of their case, were without work. Four others had no home to which to go if released. They ranged in appearance from an unusually attractive young woman of twenty-five, in whose behalf officers of the Court had already appealed to me, so out of place did she seem among the others, to the wife of a policeman who, though the mother of twelve children, had become an outcast.

My first resolve was that I would rescue the one who seemed to be there by some unworthy trick of circumstance, but that whatever I might decide concerning the others, I would decline to accept the woman whose husband and children should have saved her ere now were such a rescue possible. My spoken answer to the judge was that I desired time to find home and employment for the women before I would take them on probation.

At the end of two days, with the assistance of a

few practical Christians,—and I may add 'that such people are coming continually to the aid of the probation office,—I was ready to accept the responsibility of the ten women. It is not possible to write of each case in detail, and so I desire to pass briefly over nine of them, and build my narrative about the one remaining.

The first case was that of a woman twenty-nine years old, married to a temperate husband engaged in a small but respectable business. She had been in a cell awaiting trial for ten weeks when I took her on probation, and I secured work for her in a private home, in order that she might escape the sociability of her old companions. She remained there only fifteen days, and was found later in a disorderly house raided by the police. I surrendered her, and she was sentenced for one year.

The second case was that of a girl seventeen years of age, a mill operative who had gone astray in a boarding house where she had engaged a room because it was cheap. Employment was obtained in a new environment, and at the end of the year she was still keeping her pledge, and had regained her self-respect.

The third case gave me a woman who had been married when a girl of fifteen years. She had begun to use liquor while her husband was serving in the army during the Spanish-American war, and upon his return he had divorced her, and her downward course had become rapid. She had served many sentences when I took her, but I found a place for her in another town, where she began life anew, and at the end of the year she was doing well.

The fourth case had certain points in common with the previous one, for the woman, a factory worker of forty-five years, who had frequently served time, told me that her intemperance dated from her desertion by her husband. She was willing to go to a distant city where her parents were living, and I permitted her to do so, and there was no subsequent record of her arrest.

The fifth woman who came to me was thirty-two years old, and likewise a mill operative, who had been convicted ten times of drunkenness. Intemperance becomes a disease in such a case, with no very reasonable prospect of a complete cure. As she must support herself, and as there was grave danger from her environment if she returned to her old haunts, I sought a factory town that prohibited the sale of liquor, and engaged a room for her there in a respectable boarding-house. I then took her from the jail where she had remained confined, and after warning her that this was her last chance for probation, gave her car-fare and told her to take the first train for the town, with the further admonition not to look behind her after she started. Several weeks later I learned that she had never left the city, and I made my search for her, and she was placed under arrest. "I was going soon," she explained; but this was not satisfactory, and she was surrendered and sentenced for one year.

When the sixth probationer, a woman of thirty-eight, told me that she was married and the mother of three children, I was attracted by her intelligence, which was above the grade of the women who had preceded her. She was an American, who at the time of her marriage had brought her husband some property; but he had turned out to be a gambler and a drinker, and her money was soon squandered, and her life became unhappy and her existence somewhat precarious, since her husband would not work. Discouragement drove her to liquor, but a sentence to forty-five days in the workhouse had caused her pride to reassert itself, and she had appealed from the sentence of the police court judge. She accepted probation eagerly, kept her pledge, and lived to see her children grow to manhood and fill good positions in the community. The husband found his natural course to a prison, larceny having followed his intemperate habits.

The seventh woman was thirty-nine years old, a factory employee, married, and with a record of ten previous convictions. This of itself was sufficient to warn me that her case was all but hopeless, and yet I permitted the woman to return to her husband. It was not a home to which she went, but a room in a lodging-house. There is something almost hopeless in the life of the woman of this age whose husband can not support her, but who must labor to pay her own board. Life holds for her fewer joys than temptations. She made no report to me beyond the fact that she had gone to work, and soon after she wrote that she was leaving the city. Yet four months later I found her in a lodging-house from which complaints had been received by the police, and prepared to surrender her to the Court. She pleaded so hard to be given still another opportunity to reform that I allowed her to go before a priest and take the pledge for one year. Her husband witnessed the act, and promised to stand by her. But it was all in vain. While she had the desperation of an animal at bay in seeking to retain her freedom, she was without will power when the craving for alcohol possessed her, and on the following day she was under arrest for drunkenness and disorderly conduct. Her only request was that she might be sent away without the knowledge of the probation officer, and she stood with bowed head while the judge sentenced her to Sherborn for one year, the very period of the pledge that she had failed to keep.

The eighth case was one of quite unusual features. The woman, thirty years old, had been ruined at the age of nineteen, and had been turned out of doors by her parents. She was deserted by the father of her child, and when the latter died came to Massachusetts from Canada with a married couple of her acquaintance. But she fell in love with this man, and he left his own wife to elope with her, and they had lived together for two years when the police broke up their home. She was under arrest and the man was a fugitive from justice; and under the circumstances probation seemed as reasonable as to imprison her for the sins of the two. I sent her to New Hampshire to work, with the agreement not to seek to rejoin her lover. Almost at once, however, she began to write to him, begging him to gain the right to marry her, and declaring that she could never find happiness otherwise. The domestic tangle looked well-nigh hopeless, when assistance came from an unexpected quarter. The wife, realizing that the husband no longer loved her, offered to divorce him; and thus freed, he ultimately married my probationer, and they have lived an apparently happy life these several years.

And this brings me to the ninth woman and the patrolman's wife; the mother of twelve children, with a record of fifteen court convictions; deserted by her entire family because she had become the victim of a curse that spares not even motherhood. Upon three occasions before she had been released upon probation without avail; yet she came to herself on this last chance, and for the six remaining years of her life was a repentant woman, reunited with her family.

So I come now to the case of Marcia Brown.   It was no ordinary case, as I learned from my first frank talk with her.   Her life was ruined while she was a pupil in the High School of a New Hampshire city, and the man who accomplished her downfall was a lawyer, and a friend of her family.   He enticed her to his office on the plea of aiding her in her studies, and he assumed no responsibility for her after she became a mother.   He is dead now, and so can not read this story of her life.   For that fact I am sorry.

The girl's parents, judging her by rigorous standards, closed their door upon her when the disgrace became known, and so shut her out of their lives. At seventeen, her child dead, she went to work in the neighboring city of Concord to earn her livelihood.

She was not the type of girl, nor was hers the age to be so cast adrift without a father's protection and a mother's advice.   For seven months she stood up against the temptations that began to dog her footsteps; and then she fell.   She went so low that she became a common thing of the brothels, haled before the court in that first year of her mad recklessness, arrested eleven times in the nine years that followed, sent several times to jails and reformatories.

I cite these facts to indicate the problem that confronted me when, appealing from her latest sentence, and already sobered and restored to outward respectability by her confinement awaiting trial, she lined up with the ten women whom the judge set apart for an experiment in probation.

Although she had appealed from the lower court, and consequently had not begun to serve the sentence imposed upon her, she had been an inmate of a cell for four months and twenty-three days on that day when they finally brought her into court. Her face betrayed no emotion when her case and that of the other women was put over until later in the week; but in my office two days later, assured of an opportunity to go back into the world, she flung herself at full length upon the floor, and with her face buried in her arms, sobbed in uncontrolled emotion.

I took that girl into my own home, where my wife, so often my confidant in desperate cases involving women, brought her back to a sane view of life. We told her that there was still a chance to begin anew, with the slate wiped clean, but that it must be done in a community where she was not known. At the end of a week I had secured a place for her in the home of a wealthy family a hundred miles away; and the woman who took her knew her whole story, and accepted the trust with no false ideas concerning it.

It is wonderful how a woman will develop when she is back in her proper world. Marcia Brown, after a few months of clean living, would have passed as the social equal of the people who had befriended her. Indeed, upon one occasion, they took her, gowned as they were dressed, to one of the great balls of the state, where she attracted the attention of the Governor, who invited her to dance with him. Back and forth they glided over the polished floor, the chief executive of an important state, and the girl who had been a Magdalene; and when I heard of it, I felt that the fight was won, and that there would be no further danger from the undertow of the Underworld.

One day she wrote me that she desired to become self-supporting, and had secured employment with a manufacturing company. This would have given me some apprehension, had I not also learned that a young mechanic of good repute was keeping company with her, and that his suit was favored.

Marcia Brown was promoted in a short time to be the forewoman of her department. She was working now for her future home, and the date of her marriage had been set. How often has marriage proven the salvation of the woman of damaged reputation!

That was a winter of desperately cold weather

and frequent snowstorms. On one of the worst nights the man who was to make Marcia Brown his wife started to go from the town where he lived to a village a few miles away, a business errand calling him there. He did not return, and on the following day his frozen body was found beside the road in a bleak, wind-blown bit of country. He had perished in the storm.

I wish that I might have been there to have broken the news to the girl. Fate had kicked the prop out from under her, and now stood mocking like a very devil, ironical as to what she would do. At first she seemed to bear up very well. The full force of the shock did not reach her until the body was laid away in the ground. Not many days later a long distance telephone call summoned me to her aid.

It was a Marcia Brown disheveled, hysterical and rebellious that I found; and the details of her latest experience threw another sidelight upon the temptations that one may meet in a seemingly safe environment. She had fought against her despair until, becoming desperate at her loss, she had sought liquor to drown her sorrow. The only method by which it could be obtained was a purchase for medicinal use at a drugstore. Flushed with excitement, pretty even in her grief, she entered an apothecary's and demanded liquor.

The clerk gave her an appraising look. He had

seen her before, and he had wondered whether, at some time in her life, she had not been other than what she now appeared. His manner was ingratiating and friendly as he produced the bottle. He invited her to go to ride with him as soon as he could close the shop.

Marcia went. She returned later, noisy and insolent of what the world might think of her. Again a man had entered her life to lead her astray; though but a sordid little drug clerk, who would go on his careless way without remembering that he was contributing to her downfall. I went to the factory and drew the $49 due her, and told the manufacturer that she was going away. He was an honorable man, with a full knowledge of the world and its temptations, and he urged me to send her back to work, believing that she would right herself. But I knew better than that.

On the way to Boston she asked me to return her to prison. "Two years ago I might have been saved, but now it is too late," she said.

"It is never too late, and you've got to make good because I have vouched for you," I said. "We will find work in a new place, and begin all over again."

In Boston she expressed a wish to purchase articles of clothing that she might need, and I shopped with her. She asked to be allowed to dine at a chop house of none too respectable repute, where she had once known the old crowd, and we went there, even at the risk of my own reputation. I felt that she was putting me to the test, and that it was important that her mood should have its run. Where to obtain work for her I did not know until, my eye scanning the want columns of a newspaper, I noted that girls were wanted for work in a shoe factory in an adjacent city.

We called there two hours later, and the manager turned us down. He was sorry, but he had just engaged the last girl needed.

"You have simply got to make room for one more," I said.

"Oh, I have," he replied.

"You have, for the case is one of need that warrants it," I told him.

"Very well. Send her in tomorrow."

I found Marcia a boarding-place with a widow, and I bought her an alarm clock for fear that she might sleep over-time.

"You could not have done more for me had I been your own daughter," she said with gratitude as I left her.

"Show me that you appreciate it," I answered. "You know that I have sworn to keep you out of jail."

She wrote to me once a fortnight for a time; and then the letters ceased. I went at once to look her up, and the widow met me at the door. "She is gone," she exclaimed. "It is dreadful."

I surmised that she had learned the young woman's story, though I had been careful to conceal my identity, and asked her to tell me what had happened.

"She came in the other night showing the effects of liquor," she said. "She had told me all about herself before, and how you had tried to help her. I had come to love her already, because I have had trouble of my own, and understood. But she came to me on this night and said that her case was hopeless, and that she was going to the devil, where she belonged. I followed her out to the sidewalk with my arms about her, pleading for her to return. I was ready to do anything to help her. But she would not come back."

"We'll bring her back," I said.

I traced her to the old city of Gloucester, by the sea, but she slipped from me there. When she discovered that I was upon her trail she left me the message: "Don't follow me any more. It's no use. I am a lost woman."

But still I kept up the search for a time, until I learned that she had left the state.

"Well, and how did your ten women turn out?" inquired the judge at the end of the year.

"Indifferently well," I replied; and gave him the details. Five of them had rendered a good account of themselves. Another had shown improved behavior. Three had been surrendered and sentenced.

Five years passed, and I looked into the record of these women again, to see what had become of them. Three were permanently lost now in crime, one had died, three continued to give a good account of themselves, and three could be credited with showing improved behavior. For I had found Marcia Brown. She was married, to a man established in business, and able to give her a good home. He was not of her own race; but what of that! She was no longer a thing to be buffeted about the world; and from that day to now I have heard no word of evil spoken against her.

What of this experiment, then? We obtained some salvage, and on the basis of the results many a woman since then has been given one more chance, even in the face of a record that did not always seem to warrant it. We have not saved all thus taken; but if we have kept one in every two permanently out of our corrective institutions, it has been worth while.

"For," as the judge said, "these institutions do not reform." The problem is too great for them. It is not that they are not well managed, or that the State behind them does not earnestly desire to redeem its citizens who have gone astray.

It is the same State that has introduced the system of probation and of parole, hoping thereby to rescue even a few. It is the same State that will abolish all penal institutions when a way can be found to check crime and protect the Commonwealth in some better manner.

CHAPTER XX

The time inevitably came, in the writing of this book, when I sought the significant incident or the compelling phrase to introduce its closing chapter. Neither occurred to me at the moment, and yet both were to be forthcoming within the week. For another fall term of the court opened, with its wealth of new experiences, and its further accumulation of evidence bearing on probation.

The business of the session was no more than under way, when the judge upon the bench sent for me and stated that he desired me to occupy a position within speaking distance of him during the trial of the cases, an intimate nearness that would serve to make me the spokesman in behalf of any defendant of whom good could be said.

It was not until I had returned to my office late in the day that the significance of that incident came over me. It was not myself that the judge had thus placed between himself and the prisoners at the bar, but the Probation System of Massachusetts. We had come at last to the point where the Court was willing to risk a defendant upon probation wherever it was possible, whereas we had begun, those many years back, by granting it only in the case that promised an exceptional opportunity for reform.

I sat down to review in my own mind the progress that this movement had made in the present young century. Prior to the year 1899 Massachusetts alone had authorized the use of probation; and now in 1915 adult probation laws were in force in twenty-five states, and juvenile probation had been established in forty-three. And since this was so, but with Massachusetts still remaining in the lead, —for this is the only state that has extended the system to every county, and permits no criminal offender to be sentenced until there has been a friendly investigation on the part of a probation officer,—it seemed fair to me to summarize the story that this book has attempted to tell, and to draw from its experiences some conclusions that might contribute to the advancement of probation work.

I returned anew to this task of writing; and as I did so, there flashed through my mind the phrase that I had been seeking—"Reformatories without walls." Here, in three words, is the conclusion of the whole matter. It is to this climax that I have been working from the beginning of the first chapter. We are not striving to condone crime in Massachusetts. But we are seeking to bring men back to their senses and to a real knowledge of their guilt, in prisons that have no walls!

I carried this thought to Mr. Herbert C. Parsons, the deputy commissioner of our Commission on Probation, an executive officer of unquestioned integrity of purpose, and one who has an abiding faith in the inherent good that still survives in men and women who have gone astray. He serves an unpaid board of five members, all of whom are keenly alert to this problem of human salvage. I spoke to him of the reformatories without walls, and I said further:

"But have we come to the point where we can honestly say that we have created them by probation? Has it gone so far beyond the experimental stage that we can argue fully concerning it?"

"I understand what you mean," he replied. "We have indeed reached that point, though perhaps we can claim to have come to it only in this year."

He drew from his desk a sheet of paper upon which appeared the totals of all the men and women who had been found guilty of offenses against the Commonwealth within twelve months, with the disposition of their cases. For the first time in the history of the State—very likely in the history of the world,—more than 50 per cent. of the lawbreakers of Massachusetts who had been found guilty were at liberty, but under probation supervision. We had placed only 49 per cent. of them within prisons that had visible walls!

The fact was of such tremendous significance that

I almost forgot to translate it into comparative figures that would strengthen the appeal. My own mind was quite willing to pause at the knowledge that we were now figuratively saving more than one man out of every two for special treatment under the new theory of human salvage.

Yet it can be so translated. On the one hand we have a probation system that employs 134 men and women at an annual cost of $148,000, and they work for the reformation of 51 per cent. of the men and women who otherwise would be committed to cells. It is a system more than self-sustaining, since these probation officers also collect $300,000 in the course of the year, to be applied to court expenses, purposes of restitution and reparation, and in non-support or illegitimate child cases.

On the other hand, we have a penal system that requires 734 officers to guard and instruct the 49 per cent. of the prisoners that remain; and the cost is $2,000,000 a year in round numbers.

I offer these figures only by way of comparative argument. We shall find, of course, certain offsetting items to be credited to the institutions with walls, because in addition to the manufactured articles that they produce, there are the trades taught to those who have been living by their wits, and there is the supervision that aims to restore men without the law to normal citizenship. But since, until so very recently, we were giving all guilty men and women the more costly treatment, though we knew it to be without results, is it not fair to argue, for the benefit of those states that still hesitate to accept the doctrine of probation, that as a dollar-and-cents proposition here is a reform that justifies itself in the opinion of the tax-payer, even when one takes no account of the humanitarian principles involved?

One must not make the mistake of presuming that men continue in the business of being criminals chiefly because we send them to prison, or that all evil-doers who are given one more chance to reform will accept it gladly, and henceforth become law-abiding, constructive citizens. What I offered as my premise in the beginning, I repeat here. There are three classes of men who commit crime: the professionals, who have chosen a life of crime because they believe, in spite of all evidence to the contrary, that it offers them an easy living commensurate to the risk of arrest and punishment involved; second, the defectives, who cannot keep within the law, because they are either abnormal or subnormal; and third, the accidental and occasional offenders, who may be saved if to them is offered reform through probation, rather than a punishment that will scar them with the mark of time-server.

Thomas Mott Osborne has written of the new idea of imprisonment:

"The old barbaric theory which regarded the treatment of criminals as a matter of retribution and punishment, is gradually giving way to the civilized theory of reformation and education. Yet it remains a fact that our whole system of criminal law is still based upon that old and hateful theory. The first duty of a prison reformer, therefore, is to impress and reimpress upon the public the doctine that the present theory of the law must be changed,—that its aim should never be punishment, but prevention and reform. The prison system now endeavors to make men industrious by driving them to work; to make them virtuous by removing temptation; to make them respect the law by forcing them to obey the edicts of authority; to make them far-sighted by allowing them no chance to exercise foresight; to give them individual initiative by treating them in large groups; in short to prepare them again for society by placing them in conditions as unlike real society as they could well be made."

To this new creed many states already have subscribed, while others are watching with critical interest the experiments under way in New York and Massachusetts. Yet one must make record here of the important fact that creed alone is not a panacea. Any prison and any probation system may be wrecked by turning it over to the politicians. The success of probation depends in the first instance upon the appointive power of the judges, and their ability to select men and women who are actuated by a higher motive than a desire for official position and the income to be derived from it. One almost hesitates to use a phrase often misunderstood, that probation work calls for the highest Christian service—not the "God bless you, go and sin no more" type, but the willingness to find a man a boarding-place and employment, and the charity to discount in advance the stumbling-blocks that are certain to appear in his way.

It is possible to be an excellent police officer, and still make an unsuccessful probation officer. The point of view is not the same; and this is best illustrated by the fact that before probation came into use the prisoner at the bar was always confronted by the prosecuting police official, who offered as evidence the record of his past misdemeanors. The law, acting in all honesty, and from a desire to protect the community, spoke all the ill that could be said against a defendant. Under a more enlightened system, the probation officer may offset this by making known such mitigating circumstances as he may have discovered; an environment leading to crime, dishonesty impelled by the pressure of debt, offenses committed under the stimulus of drugs or alcohol, repentance and remorse shown while in jail awaiting trial.

And again, it is possible to be an honest probation officer, but a lax one. Any state that develops the system as far as Massachusetts has gone is ultimately confronted by the need of trained supervision, to the end that a high standard, once established, may be evenly maintained. It is not possible for one deputy commissioner to administer a department growing so rapidly, and still find the time that he might desire to check up the detailed work of the several counties, in order that he may know whether all cases are followed up intelligently, and be assured that the best judgment is used in the peculiar problems that are certain to arise from time to time. In Massachusetts there has been developed a wonderfully loyal group of men and women, the best among them real missioners in their desire to save the victims of temptation or folly; yet none of them would question the right of the state to audit their human salvage accounts as carefully as those involving the money they receive and pay out.

Certain Western States, at the present time, are advocating the appointment of an official sometimes referred to as the people's lawyer. He is to be an attorney paid by the government and available to all defendants when they are on trial. To my own mind, this is not the step forward that it may appear to be. Quite likely I am mistaken in my judgment, since it is based only upon conditions as I find them in Massachusetts. Each state has its own problems, and what I am about to say is not to be accepted as an argument against a reform that has able advocates supporting it. I would merely offer the suggestion that the ideal probation system should make the defendant's attorney unnecessary. The true probation officer is the people's lawyer, and he is not seeking to make a record of non-convictions. In a murder trial the prisoner at the bar already has competent counsel provided for him at the expense of the state. The theory is that the law, assuming the accused to be innocent until it proves him guilty, stands ready to safeguard his every right in the face of the forces that it is prepared to bring against him.

In practice this often works out quite otherwise. One group of lawyers is pitted against another, each exerting every turn and twist of the law to secure a conviction or an acquittal, while the newspapers develop interest in the trial until it becomes little less than a sporting event. Permit such contests to extend to all criminal trials, even to a minor degree, and courts would be obliged to sit twelve months in the year, and ultimately include the Sabbath day in order to clear their dockets.

No, it is far better to send to the prisoner's cell the probation officer who may gain his confidence, if not, indeed, secure a confession from him. If there is any mitigating circumstance for the man who makes a clean breast of his crime, the probation officer suggests a plea of guilty and agrees to take him on probation, with the consent of the court. The first step toward reformation is for an accused man to tell the truth, and it is better for him to throw himself upon the clemency of the judge with an admission of guilt, than to contest the case with a lie upon his lips. Since it costs, on an average, $300 a day to run our county courts in Massachusetts, the settlement of scores of cases without a lengthy trial saves a large sum of money at every session of the court, and works for justice to all concerned, rather than otherwise. Better a guilty prisoner repentant and on probation, than one who, by the aid of an ingenious lawyer, is technically found not guilty when he himself knows that justice has been tricked.

Probation, I repeat, is no panacea. It will not pull down all prison walls. But it has brought us, nevertheless, to a consideration of whether our reformatories should not be a clearing-house for all persons convicted of felonies and misdemeanors, rather than a concentration camp of men who are not all amenable to reform. Judges do not all look upon crime with equal severity or leniency. In the more sparsely settled country, where townspeople are law-abiding to a marked degree, a defendant may receive a stiff sentence in unconscious deference to public opinion, whereas the same crime committed in a city would be considered with greater leniency. Possibly the time has come to give the

Prison Commission, in such a state as Massachusetts, authority to classify the men committed to the Reformatory, transferring to the prison those who have served prison sentences in other states, committing to a House of Correction the occasional cases that might better be handled there, removing the subnormal to a camp for indefinite detention, and retaining those who appear to be the real material for permanent reform.

One may properly inquire as to how judges themselves view probation. During my service as a probation officer I have worked under twenty-eight of them, and I have found them universally of one opinion.

"Probation defined is but practical Christianity," observed Chief Justice John A. Aiken one day.

"The only persons we save nowadays are those we do not send to prison," said Judge Edgar J. Sherman.

"The system of probation is a departure from the theory of punishment advocated by penologists," was the conclusion of the late Judge Daniel W. Bond. "It is more in accordance with the injunction 'Go and sin no more.'"

Judge Frederick Lawton, in placing a youth on probation one cold winter's day, learned that he was without home, occupation, or suitable clothing. One of the jurors offered to employ the young man, and the judge promptly directed the probation officer to purchase the necessary wearing apparel, adding: "And if there are no funds to meet the cost, pass the bill over to me."

Judge Marcus Morton, while presiding at a session of the Superior Criminal Court, one day left the bench and went over to where the mother of a young delinquent was sitting, in order to question her and the better understand the environment of the defendant.

Judge George A. Sanderson's administration of probation has always disclosed an intimate understanding of the men who come before him for sentence, and this may be due to the fact that while district attorney, the prosecuting officer of the county, he was accustomed to drive several miles on a Sunday in order to teach a Sunday School class at the Reformatory.

So one might go on through the entire list, and find its counterpart in the other counties. I have seen tears in the eyes of more than one justice when he has been compelled to impose a sentence in a case where probation could not be given, though it offered some mitigating circumstance. And it is from such men that the Governor selects those who administer the probation laws. Justice Charles A. DeCourcey, prior to his appointment to the Supreme Bench, was chairman of the Commission on Probation, and he in turn was succeeded by a former judge, Hon. Robert O. Harris. To have made appointments to this commission a reward for political service would have been second only to giving the selection of probation officers over to the politicians. It is well not to lose sight of these facts in any state where probation is under contemplation.

While a majority of the States now have probation laws, as yet there is no Federal legislation, although the National Probation Association has twice sought to obtain it. The United States District Courts try over 13,000 criminal cases annually, and it is estimated that 80 per cent. of these are first offenders. And it is among such that the human salvage of the courts is to be found. Those of us who look hopefully to the future see not only this Federal legislation, but a standardization of the work of the juvenile courts, and a supervision of probation in all states by competent commissions.

Have I made out my case for probation? Strangely enough, I find at the bottom of my heart less a desire to convince those of you who may never have need of it, than I do those others, their number legion, who are straying from the path of sane, honest living, or who are already at odds with the law. Not in vain has been the labor of this book if its appeal reaches to their secret heart. I am not pleading with them on behalf of the law or society at large. I do not offer as an argument for their going straight the forces of the trained police, the prosecuting officers and the experienced judges, nor the traps set for them by the finger-print system.

I only ask them to draw from the true stories that I have related the conclusion that the game itself will inevitably beat them in the end. For the game is "rigged." It does not offer them one chance in a hundred to win in the end. Lawlessness as a business proposition does not pay.

Such witnesses as I would summon to convince them are young Kenwood, Charles Tower, Thomas Bullock, Luigi Salvadore, and Marcia Brown. These are real men and women, though to shield them from publicity, I have cloaked them in ficti-tious names. You have seen their temptations, their struggles, their victories, and in some cases their defeats. To me they are real; and as I sometimes walk the streets of Boston, and Cambridge, and Lowell, and a dozen other cities and towns by night, they step out unexpectedly from the crowd to greet me, and we grasp hands suddenly, to exchange frank and hearty greetings ere we part. Thank God for such meetings as those!

THE END